"Richard Schultz has produce
cussion of some of the wrong t
Scripture. While he rightfully
properly desire to apply these
also tries to guide lay readers a.
complish the same task when their attempts go wrong. This book is a delightful read that will bring both tears and outbursts of laughter as examples of poor interpretations are shared. Here is a book that is a must for all readers of the Bible, which I recommend for each person's enlightenment and enjoyment."

Walter C. Kaiser Jr., president emeritus,
Gordon-Conwell Theological Seminary

"Having a correct view of God and living a faithful life are dependent on hearing God's voice accurately, and Schultz helps sort out the good, the bad, and the ugly in the world of interpretation and application. He exposes the inherent danger of misusing Scripture and leads us into a more careful approach to interpreting and applying Scripture in a way that is faithful to the text's original meaning and context. This book will help wean us off of the false conclusions of sloppy interpretation and will help us sort out the confusion that is so prevalent in so many Christian circles. It is a book that will inspire and teach at the same time, leading us to hunger and thirst for God's Word all the more."

Eric J. Bargerhuff, author of *The Most Misused Verses in the Bible: Surprising Ways God's Word Is Misunderstood*

"The authority of the Bible is under attack from many quarters today. Sadly, much of this is the result of self-inflicted wounds—Christians misreading and misapplying God's Word. Richard Schultz's *Out of Context* is a clarion call for greater attention to the meaning of the text in its original context. His dozens of examples from popular Christian literature provide not only warnings against the errors of the past but also positive principles for gleaning God's truth from Scripture today. This is must reading for Christian teachers, preachers, and writers."

Mark L. Strauss, professor of New Testament, Bethel Seminary San Diego; author of *How to Read the Bible in Changing Times: Understanding and Applying God's Word Today*

"*Out of Context* is a readable, understandable, and persuasive plea for Christians in all walks of life to raise the standard of biblical interpretation by demanding it in the books we read and providing it in the books we write and publish."

Julie Ackerman Link, editor, author, Bible study leader

"We hear God's voice in Scripture when we interpret it correctly. Nothing could be more important. Richard Schultz masterfully guides us away from common mistakes of interpretation and toward a reading that will transform our minds and hearts. This book is must reading for all Christians."

Tremper Longman III, Robert H. Gundry Professor
of Biblical Studies, Westmont College

"*Out of Context* is a practical guide to important skills for interpreting the Bible—practical enough to encourage you that growth as a student of Scripture is really possible. Richard Schultz also offers a good example of truly constructive criticism: his treatment of problematic interpretations is humble, restrained, and forward-looking, helping readers not just to see what's wrong but also to pursue what's right. This book therefore models the harmony of truth and love we need to see more often in the body of Christ."

Daniel J. Treier, professor of theology, Wheaton College; author
of *Introducing Theological Interpretation of Scripture*

"*Out of Context* is an important book written by a careful Bible scholar who loves the church and understands the issues people face as we seek to hear God's Word and respond to it in our world. Before I had read fifty pages, I thought to myself, 'This man longs for people to hear authentically what God is saying in his Word—not just what they hope God is saying in his Word.' By the time I finished, I was convinced that *Out of Context* does more than demonstrate how we often misread and misapply Scripture. It also provides real help to enable us to interpret it and live faithfully in keeping with its message.

"I should add one more point: the book is very readable. That makes it a book I want not only my pastoral colleagues but all my church people to read. It's evident that Dr. Schultz knows how to make complex issues concise and clear. I especially appreciate the chapter on how genre influences meaning. I'll be recommending this book to pastors and lay teachers—indeed, to all who want to listen to, understand, and obey God's Word."

Greg Waybright, PhD, senior pastor, Lake Avenue Church,
Pasadena, CA

"To any who interact regularly with the Bible but especially to those who minister God's Word—pastors, teachers, authors—and who desire to share it with others in a fresh and living way without dishonoring God by mishandling his Word, this book will be very useful as both guide and guardrail. Schultz's identification of specific 'mishandlings' and his use of concrete examples makes his book particularly helpful. I commend it highly."

Mike Bullmore, senior pastor, CrossWay
Community Church, Bristol, WI

Out of Context

How to Avoid Misinterpreting the Bible

RICHARD L. SCHULTZ

BakerBooks

a division of Baker Publishing Group
Grand Rapids, Michigan

Published by Baker Books
a division of Baker Publishing Group
P.O. Box 6287, Grand Rapids, MI 49516-6287
www.bakerbooks.com

Printed in the United States of America

Library of Congress Cataloging-in-Publication Data

Schultz, Richard L.
    Out of context : how to avoid misinterpreting the Bible / Richard L. Schultz.
        p.   cm.
    Includes bibliographical references (p.   ).
    ISBN 978-0-8010-7228-4 (pbk.)
    1. Bible—Hermeneutics. I. Title.
BS476.S345 2012
220.601—dc23   2012013686

In keeping with biblical principles of creation stewardship, Baker Publishing Group advocates the responsible use of our natural resources. As a member of the Green Press Initiative, our company uses recycled paper when possible. The text paper of this book is composed in part of post-consumer waste.

12   13   14   15   16   17   18   7   6   5   4   3   2   1

Contents

Introduction

Why I Am Swatting the Beehive
When I Know It Will Upset the Bees

Have you ever sat in the stands at a sporting event or in front of your television while a game was being broadcast with the score tied and time running out? The game-deciding play was set up—and executed poorly. And your team lost! Your immediate response may have been to yell (perhaps at the television), telling the athletes what they should have done. After all, you have played the sport yourself, so you should know.

My experience as a professional student and teacher of the Bible has been similar. Through years of in-depth training and nearly three decades of studying the Scriptures and teaching students how to interpret them well, I have become increasingly aware of how frequently Christian writers—as well as secular politicians—use the Bible. I have noticed that sometimes they use it well, but far too often they use it poorly. And in the latter case, like the sports fan, I wish I could tell them what they should have done. It's not just a matter of taste and familiarity—like when I find it difficult to get used to a favorite hymn that I grew up singing with organ accompaniment now being played by the worship band with a very different rhythm and tempo. Rather, these writers understand Bible phrases or individual verses in ways that are contrary to their original meaning, suggesting meanings that the wording and immediate context of the text do not support, meanings not found in any standard commentary.

Sometimes these Bible interpreters read contemporary concerns, values, associations, and word usage into the ancient biblical text. And often that misinterpretation is accompanied by misapplication. At other times they claim a promise made in a very specific situation to one individual in ancient times as if God had delivered it personally to them. Or they view themselves and their readers as another Moses figure. For example, their problems with an ungrateful and rebellious teenager are treated as virtually identical to Moses's struggle with the recently liberated but murmuring Israelites who voted to head back to beautiful Egypt. Admittedly, what counts as an appropriate application and what is far-fetched may to some extent be a matter of opinion, but it is fair to ask in such a case what basis the interpreter has for making such an application.[1]

I began to notice misinterpretation and misuse everywhere: not only in popular Christian books but also in blog posts, Christian magazines, radio broadcasts, sermons, and adult Sunday school lessons. They began buzzing around me like bees at a muggy July picnic, seemingly taunting me, until I had to take a swat at them. The first swat came in April 1997 at the annual theology conference cosponsored by Wheaton College and InterVarsity Press. In a paper I critiqued a series of misused texts that I had found in various Christian self-help books by well-known evangelical authors. This led to an invitation to express my concerns in a workshop at the annual Christian Book Editors Conference in March 1998 and a much later invitation to suggest a "solution" to the problem at a conference cosponsored by the Society for Christian Psychology and the American Association of Christian Counselors in September 2008.

In the meantime, a former biblical interpretation student of mine, then one of the leaders of a Christian parachurch ministry, emailed me, asking if I had read Bruce Wilkinson's bestselling *The Prayer of Jabez* (2000). Every employee of his organization had been given a copy of that small book to read, and he was disturbed by Wilkinson's interpretation and application of an obscure verse from 1 Chronicles. After reading the book I was equally disturbed and wrote a brief critique. The resulting article, originally intended for the Wheaton College student newspaper, ended up being published in *Trinity Journal* in 2003. Finally, a few years ago, I decided that it was time to swat the beehive, writing a full-length book to further expose the widespread and blatant misuse of Scripture by bestselling Christian authors.

It is my conviction that the Bible often suffers as much abuse at the hands of its friends as at the hands of its enemies, and I feel the need to do something about it. I realize that some of my readers will consider my efforts to be at best nitpicky, or at worst loveless. Some of the authors cited here might take the time to dispute my claims, but this book is unlikely to reduce the sales of their books. Too many Christian readers are blissfully unaware of the issues I will address *ignorance?* below. They will buy and read what others recommend. And if they are blessed by a book's contents, it has to be right, doesn't it? How many churches are systematically teaching their members to be careful readers of Scripture? More often they encourage them to participate in the type of Bible studies that sometimes promote rather than reduce misinterpretation.

My goal in this book is not to dwell on what I consider to be the interpretive errors of others but rather to use them, beginning with *The Prayer of Jabez*, as negative examples as I set forth guidelines for properly understanding the Bible. I am not seeking to offer a complete guide to personal Bible study; many such guides are already available. I will focus instead on three central features of biblical texts—literary context, individual words, and literary genres (chapters 3–5). Then I will give detailed attention to the difficult task of moving from interpretation to application (chapter 6). But because of my focus on the interpretive errors of others, I will begin and end the book with lengthy treatments of why and how Christians misinterpret the Bible (chapters 1–2) and why this needs to be corrected (chapter 7). I will have succeeded if this book causes those who read it to begin evaluating how Scripture is used all around them and to seek out a more comprehensive guide to biblical interpretation to learn more.

I am grateful to Baker Books for the opportunity to put my concerns in print for a wider audience. D. A. Carson's *Exegetical Fallacies*, also published by Baker (2nd ed., 1996), has been an inspiration and a model for me in preparing this book. Bob Hosack has been a patient and encouraging editor, believing in the importance of what I am presenting and in my ability to present it effectively. I have re-used some materials from previous publications in this book. A more technical version of my critique of Bruce Wilkinson's *The Prayer of Jabez* appeared in *Trinity Journal* as "Praying Jabez's Prayer: Turning an Obscure Biblical Narrative into a Miracle-Working Mantra."[2] Some of the examples of misinterpretation included in chapters 3–5 appeared in "Responsible Hermeneutics for Wisdom Literature," in *Care for the Soul: Exploring the Intersection of Psychology and Theology*, edited by M. R. McMinn and T. R. Phillips,[3] or in "'For I did not shrink from declaring to you the whole purpose of God': Biblical Theology's Role within Christian Counseling," in *Edification: The Transdisciplinary Journal of Christian Psychology*.[4]

My examples of faulty interpretation and application are drawn from a wide range of authors and publishers (including a few published by Baker). Although I have sought to use as many examples as possible from books and articles published during the past few decades, some go back as far as the 1970s. There are three reasons for this. First of all, I wish to demonstrate that this is not a new problem but an old one. (I suppose I could have gone all the way back to some of the interpreters of the early church!) Second, I wanted to use some of the books that were influential in my Christian life during my early adult years when I was in seminary and then took my first faltering steps as a young interim pastor of three different churches. I assume that these books have been influential in the lives of some of my readers as well. Finally, some of the examples were "discovered" on the dusty shelves of the Wheaton College library by students in my biblical interpretation course, which I have now taught for sixteen years. In a brief paper, they were required to do with one text what I have done with many—to critique and correct an author's use of Scripture. Occasionally their analyses served to correct my own past misuse of specific texts.

I am grateful for my students' company on my hermeneutical journey. I am always encouraged when alumni tell me that they continue to use what they learned in my course and to share it with others. This book is dedicated to them and to my wife, Carol, who has accompanied me on this journey for more than three decades. Over the years, she and I have discussed numerous examples of misused biblical texts, including many that she has discovered. She too is a student and teacher of the Word and has encouraged me to write this book. A number of student research assistants have contributed to the categorization of examples or to the proofreading of the manuscript. These include Brandon Levering, Laura Lysen, Hamille Chou, Steven Dunkel, and Brittany Kim. Brittany is now a biblical scholar in her own right, and her careful editing of my work has made it more coherent and readable. It has been our goal and prayer as we have worked together on this project that the church, which values God's Word so highly, will honor its author by reading and using it with greater care.

1

The "Jabez Prayer" Phenomenon

Flunking Biblical Interpretation 101

Christians buy (and hopefully read) a lot of books. Perhaps this helps to explain why a number of books with an explicit faith focus have landed on the *New York Times* bestsellers list, such as *90 Minutes in Heaven* by Don Piper and the Tim LaHaye–Jerry Jenkins Left Behind series. But who would have thought that a brief exposition of an obscure verse plucked from the midst of nine chapters of boring "begats" could scale those lofty heights?

That is precisely what happened to Bruce Wilkinson's *The Prayer of Jabez: Breaking Through to the Blessed Life*, which was published in 2000.[1] After hearing a chapel message on 1 Chronicles 4:10 while a seminarian and praying and preaching the prayer for nearly three decades, Wilkinson, of "Walk thru the Bible" fame, decided that it was time to publish his thoughts on the prayer. The results were staggering: the book sold more than eight million copies in the first year and was declared by *Publishers Weekly* "the fastest selling book of all time." Numerous Christian ministries distributed the book to their entire staff, membership, or interested broadcast listeners.

The phenomenal sales quickly spawned a cottage industry of Jabez boutique versions (for example, special versions for preschoolers, preteens, teens, and women, as well as a leather-bound copy, journal, and worship music). An expanding line of Jabez kitsch soon followed: coins, fake rocks, and wooden crosses inscribed with "The Prayer," as well as Jabez coffee mugs, bath gel, and neckties. Sadly, a proposal for Jabez candy bars was rejected because it ran the risk of "overcommercial-izing" poor Jabez! And plans for a full-length film based on the prayer of Jabez and featuring major Hollywood talent were also later scrapped.

An official Prayer of Jabez website gave scores of satisfied pray-ers a forum for sharing glowing testimonials regarding their most recent "Jabez blessings," such as healing, new property, career advancement, investment gains, or "Jabez appointments" (for example, conversa-tions). Only a few contributors complained that their Jabez prayers had not *yet* yielded any visible results. By every pragmatic measure, God was blessing Bruce Wilkinson (and his little ninety-three-page booklet) *indeed*. After all, hasn't God promised that his Word will not return to him "empty"? Will it not rather "achieve the purpose for which [he] sent it" (Isa. 55:11)?

But was the recent Prayer of Jabez phenomenon really the purpose for which a divinely inspired author included Jabez's brief prayer in 1–2 Chronicles shortly after the Jews returned from Babylonian exile? (Or could someone with Bruce Wilkinson's evangelical pedigree have just as easily turned another obscure Bible verse—or even a "fortune" found inside a Chinese restaurant cookie—into a simple prayer with comparable results?) Apart from a few negative web-based reviews and Hebrew professor Larry Pechawer's privately published *The Lost Prayer of Jabez*, Wilkinson's book received very little public criticism. Kenneth Woodward, religion reporter for *Newsweek*, however, was troubled by the tendency to turn Jabez's prayer "into a Christian mantra." In Wood-ward's opinion, virtually "any verse from the Book of Psalms, [or] the prayers Jesus himself recited, which ask only for forgiveness and the grace to do God's will" would be better choices for a widespread readership.[2]

The real problem with *The Prayer of Jabez* lies elsewhere, and it is not merely *practical* but profoundly *hermeneutical* (hermeneutics is the art and science of interpretation). In other words, Wilkinson's interpretation, application, and specific suggestions for implementing the prayer are clearly flawed. Some biblical texts are notoriously diffi-cult to understand, producing a variety of interpretive opinions (and, sometimes, speculations). Unfortunately, even seemingly clear passages are subject to misinterpretation, especially when practical concerns get in the way. Consider, for example, how easily some people (hopefully not us!) are taken in by an online or mail offer for a discounted item or service. Eager to cash in on a rare opportunity, they send it in before carefully reading the "fine print" or considering what the "catch" might be.

Similarly, we can too quickly move to claim a desirable promise or assurance in Scripture, without pausing to consider whether it really is offered to us or simply to the ancient Israelites or to the church in ancient Corinth. Let us examine the various ways in which Wilkinson's understanding of Jabez's prayer may be problematic or questionable, after briefly summarizing his book's message and claims. According to Wilkinson, the prayer recorded in 1 Chronicles 4:9–10 "contains the key to a life of extraordinary favor with God" (7). Named Jabez (meaning "Pain," according to Wilkinson) by his mother, this enterprising individual sought to counteract the ominous future that such a name anticipated by praying "the biggest, most improbable request imaginable" (22).

The Message of the Prayer of Jabez

In Wilkinson's interpretation, the four clauses of Jabez's prayer form a sequence of four distinct requests:

1. *Oh, that You would bless me indeed*: God, impart your supernatural favor, your power to accomplish great things, on me this day but do so in whatever way you desire.
2. *and enlarge my territory*: As you continue to bless me daily, grant me more influence, more responsibility, more opportunity to make an impact for you.
3. *that Your hand would be with me*: Having thus stepped out of my comfort zone and realm of personal competence, I am utterly dependent on your help if I am to succeed.
4. *and that You would keep me from evil, that I may not cause pain*: Such successes will certainly attract Satan's attack, so protect me from deception, dangerous misjudgments, or misleading feelings that could cause me to sin and thereby threaten my work for you.[3]

In sum, the prayer of Jabez, as analyzed by Wilkinson, offers a strikingly comprehensive series of requests, each of which represents a valid topic for prayer.

Problems with the Prayer of Jabez

Interpretation

What did Jabez request in his prayer and how did God respond?

Translation. Wilkinson's understanding of the prayer's fourth request is dependent on his choice of translations. Out of twenty published translations examined, only *one* supports his view, the New King James Version, for which Wilkinson served on the editorial board. The NKJV rendering, "that You would keep me from evil, that I may not cause pain," sounds strikingly similar to the final request of the Lord's Prayer. Most translations, however, understand this request quite differently:

"keep me from harm so that I will be free from pain" (NIV)

"keep me from all trouble and pain" (NLT)

"keep me from hurt and harm" (NRSV)

(The KJV's rendering, "keep *me* from evil, that it may not grieve me," is somewhat ambiguous.)

In light of the precise wording and context here, it is most likely that Jabez is requesting protection from further pain.

Sequence. According to Wilkinson, each of Jabez's four requests, in turn, must be fulfilled before the next is warranted: "Notice that Jabez did not begin his prayer by asking for God's hand to be with him. At that point, he didn't sense the need. Things were still manageable" (48). Another possibility is that there are two distinct but simultaneous two-part requests, which move from general (G) to specific (S). Such pairing of lines is typical of Hebrew elevated style and similar in structure to the high priestly blessing recorded in Numbers 6:24–26:

The Prayer of Jabez

General	Specific	
Oh, that you would bless me	and enlarge my territory!	→ More land
Let your hand be with me,	and keep me from harm so that I will be free from pain.	→ Less pain

Numbers 6:24–26

General	Specific	
The LORD bless you	and keep you;	→ Protection
the LORD make his face shine on you	and be gracious to you;	→ Favor
the LORD turn his face toward you	and give you peace.	→ Wholeness

If this alternative analysis of Jabez's prayer requests is accepted, both Wilkinson's interpretation and his subsequent application collapse.

Filling in details. Most biblical historical narratives offer a minimum of explanatory detail, focusing on the actions and words of the major characters. Thus there is a natural impulse for the reader to fill in the missing pieces of the story. This can lead, however, to a shift in emphasis from what the text actually states to what the interpreter has, often speculatively, added to the text regarding the characters' thoughts and motivations. For example, Wilkinson suggests that Jabez was "weighed down by the sorrow of his past and the dreariness of his present" (22), presumably due to his name (which sounds similar to, but does *not* mean, "pain"[4]). He claims that Jabez's request for more territory was motivated solely by his desire to "make a greater impact" for God (31).

It is more likely, however, that Jabez is simply seeking additional material resources in order to make his life easier. This is suggested by another incident recorded later in the same chapter (1 Chron. 4:38–43) in which several families from the tribe of Simeon, in search of more pastureland, destroy the non-Israelites living near the "outskirts of Gedor" in Judah and take control of their land. In addition, unlike his mother, who experienced a painful birth according to 1 Chronicles 4:9, Jabez requests that he might avoid pain in life. His prayer here may allude to Genesis 3:16–17, since these verses employ the same Hebrew root as occurs in 1 Chronicles 4:9–10 to refer to the pain of both childbirth and manual labor.

Application

What should we learn from Jabez's prayer and how should we apply it to our lives?

Turning description into prescription. Even though the Bible as an ancient Word is intended to inform and guide us in our contemporary life of faith, biblical texts do not always directly address our situation, especially since some types of texts (genres) communicate divine truths indirectly. Although Wilkinson focuses on a specific prayer attributed to a person named Jabez about whom we know very little, including when and where he lived, 1 Chronicles 4:9–10 is one of several brief anecdotes that are scattered throughout this genealogical section (chaps. 1–9) and that illustrate one of the major theological themes of 1–2 Chronicles, namely that God quickly punishes disobedience and spiritual infidelity but rewards those who trust him and seek his guidance (see, for example, 1 Chron. 5:23–26). Furthermore, Jabez's requests in 1 Chronicles 4:10 present only one of about 165 speeches (prayers, sermons, and prophetic messages) in 1–2 Chronicles.

In other words, 1 Chronicles 4:9–10 is one of many illustrations of some basic theological principles. Wilkinson, however, transforms the details of this brief historical report into a universal instruction, that is, into a *model.* Jabez's prayer is significant not because he discovered how to unlock the divine treasure trove, as Wilkinson claims, but simply because prayer is a significant subtheme in the book. Other answered prayers that, like Jabez's, address physical circumstances are found in 1 Chronicles 5:20–22; 2 Chronicles 20:6–12; 32:24. There is no textual basis for concluding, as Wilkinson does, that Jabez's prayer is more significant, either in its formulation or in its effect, than any other prayer recorded in the Bible or that he prayed it more than once or in stages.

Spiritualization. In order to make Jabez's prayer relevant to every Christian, Wilkinson also must generalize and spiritualize his request for God to "enlarge his territory" from referring to farmland (dirt!) to representing any change in our circumstances that involves "more influence, more responsibility, and more opportunity" (30). Consequently, virtually anything could qualify as an answer to this petition, including giving birth to twins, witnessing to someone on a plane, and being promoted to CEO. According to Wilkinson, praying the prayer gives you "a front row seat in a life of miracles" (44), even though it is not clear that God's original response to Jabez's prayer was miraculous by any normal definition of the term. Wilkinson also assumes that, in praying this prayer, every Christian is motivated primarily by the same desire to make a greater impact for God that he believes Jabez demonstrates, rather than by a desire for a less painful and problematic life.

Implementation

How do we go about experiencing what Jabez experienced? Here we can briefly note three of Wilkinson's questionable recommendations for implementing Jabez's prayer. (1) *Daily repetition.* Wilkinson encourages all readers to pray the prayer of Jabez daily for at least a trial month, and he recommends making this "a lifelong commitment" (29), just as he has done. (2) *Unqualified assurances.* This is linked with the promise that this is "a daring prayer that God always answers" (7). Thus, according to Wilkinson, through "a simple, believing prayer, you can change your future. You can change what happens one minute from now" (29). Such a claim could lead a person either to interpret every good thing that happens in their life as a divine answer to their prayer or to become frustrated, or even desperate, as expressed in this entry on the Prayer of Jabez website:

> I wish I had a victorious tale to tell. I am now in my 4th reading of your book since I bought it in November. I have prayed Jabez's prayer diligently, and at least once almost daily. I believe God wants to bless me. I am waiting to receive his bounty. I am still unemployed. . . . I want for nothing more than for God to show me what, if anything, is obstructing the flow of his blessings toward us. Please pray . . . for God to bless us. . . . Indeed![5]

This comment reflects (3) the *one-sided focus on personal, especially material, blessing* that characterized the Prayer of Jabez fad and needs to be balanced with a biblical desire for the kind of spiritual growth that is best fostered by difficulties in life and a call for Christian contentment.

A striking postscript illustrating the problematic nature of the Jabez prayer phenomenon has been provided by Bruce Wilkinson himself. In 2002, he moved to Africa, announcing his goal to save one million AIDS orphans through his Dream for Africa organization. He planned to establish a facility in Swaziland for ten thousand children, to be funded by a bed-and-breakfast, game reserve, Bible college, industrial park, and a Disneylike tourist resort. In October 2005, however, he abandoned his plan. According to a *Wall Street Journal* article from 2005, despite initial successes and raising half a million dollars toward his $190 million goal in 2005 alone, a combination of negative publicity, (false) accusations, and difficulties in negotiating with Swazi officials caused Wilkinson's frustrations to grow. The article concludes:

> Mr. Wilkinson says that he blames neither God nor man. He says he weeps when he thinks of his disappointed [orphan] acolytes, and is trying to come to grips with a miracle that didn't materialize despite his unceasing recitation of the Jabez prayer.
>
> "I asked hard enough," he added, his gaze drifting upward. "All we can do is ask God what to do, ask him to help us in the doing of it, and work as hard and wisely as we can. Somewhere in this it's got to be all right to attempt a vision that didn't work and not to make it an overwhelming failure."[6]

This is a startling admission from the author who promised just five years earlier that the Jabez prayer is "a daring prayer that God always answers"!

The Dilemma

In criticizing Bruce Wilkinson's use of the prayer of Jabez, I am not questioning his motivations or competence as an interpreter of the Bible. Nor am I suggesting that God would not (or did not) respond to the prayers of (some of) those sincerely praying "the prayer" at Wilkinson's encouragement. Such a well-publicized example of "enlarging" the meaning and application of the text, however, presents a serious dilemma for those charged with promoting sound biblical interpretation in the church.

Many Christians were excited to see a bestselling "biblical book" get considerable media attention, and various Christian ministries, especially Focus on the Family, enthusiastically promoted it. Since "you can't argue with success," most simply assumed that the book's success was a "God thing" and that its great impact on millions of Christians around the globe served to validate Wilkinson's "Scripture-based" assurances. Wilkinson dismissed his Christian and secular critics in a follow-up book, *Beyond Jabez*, and distanced himself from the "false teaching and preaching that surrounded the book,"[7] reaffirming his interpretation and recommending use of the Jabez prayer. Ironically, the nearly unparalleled sales of Wilkinson's little book *The Prayer of*

Jabez may tell us more about contemporary American evangelicalism than about the accuracy of Wilkinson's interpretation of Jabez's original prayer. How painful!

My seminary hermeneutics professor, Walter Kaiser, offered us an alternative explanation of much popular interpretation of Scripture: "Wonderful things in the Bible I see, most of them put there by you or by me!" He admonished us to always "keep our fingers on the text" and to become "Berean" Christians who "examined the scriptures every day to see whether these things were so" (Acts 17:11 NRSV). In the wake of the Jabez wave, I looked in vain for a renewed interest in an in-depth study of 1–2 Chronicles or of other biblical prayers. But I should not have been surprised that this never materialized. After all, Wilkinson had already discovered the *one* prayer that would unlock the heavenly storehouses and had given its definitive explanation. All that remained for Christians to do was to take his word for it and start praying the Jabez prayer themselves.

What is important to note here is that biblical interpretation can go wrong at various points. When interpreting textual details, we can adopt a questionable translation of key words or phrases. Furthermore, we can ignore both the historical and literary contexts of the passage, which largely determine how the passage should be understood and how it functions within Scripture. We can also pay too little attention to the formal, structural, and stylistic features of a text and how these shape the communication of divine truth. Further difficulties are involved in the process of application, as we bridge the gap between the world of the Bible and our contemporary world and recommend concrete steps toward affirming and living out the truths and lessons of the Scriptures. Here we can move too quickly in universalizing a specific action or instruction, assuming that what one ancient Israelite experienced can and should be experienced by all contemporary Christians.

Reasons for Misusing the Bible

Sadly, Bruce Wilkinson's hermeneutical failure is not an isolated incident. Scripture abuse permeates both our Christian and secular culture. (I will offer abundant evidence throughout this book to support this disturbing claim!) But why do sincere Christians (including me) frequently misuse biblical texts—or fail to recognize their misuse by others—despite acknowledging them to be the authoritative Word of God? In the concluding verses of his second letter, the apostle Peter offers a rather surprising answer to this question:

> So then, dear friends, since you are looking forward to this, make every effort to be found spotless, blameless and at peace with him. Bear in mind that our Lord's patience means salvation, just as our dear brother Paul also wrote you with the wisdom that God gave him. He writes the same way in all his letters, speaking in them of these matters. His letters contain some things that are hard to understand, which ignorant and unstable people distort, as they do the other Scriptures, to their own destruction. (2 Pet. 3:14–16)

After writing about God's purposes to be fulfilled in the coming destruction of the present cosmos and the creation of "a new heaven and a new earth" on the "day of the Lord" (vv. 1–13), Peter warns the recipients of his letter against being taken in by false teachers who will twist the Scriptures.

Difficulties in Interpretation

The first reason for misinterpretation that Peter mentions relates to the nature of the text itself. Peter describes some biblical texts or statements as "hard to understand." Now if the apostle Peter considered some of the writings of his fellow apostle Paul difficult to understand, we should expect much of Scripture to present us with interpretive challenges, since we are separated from the biblical authors by two to three millennia. Without the help of trained teachers and preachers and reliable books and reference tools, we are very unfamiliar with much of the culture, language, history, and literature of the Bible. Therefore, we are inclined to read biblical texts in light of our modern customs, values, and language use. The extensive diversity that we find in the Bible also complicates interpretation. We begin with the more readily understood teaching of Jesus and instructions in the letters of Paul and Peter and then expect to find equally clear statements about God's nature and purposes for us in the midst of Leviticus's laws, in the image-rich psalms, in the prophetic visions of the near and distant future, in terse proverbial sayings, and in the lengthy narratives of the history of Israel and of the early church.

But Peter reminds us that some biblical texts are inherently more difficult due to their subject matter or wording. Such texts will take more effort to understand accurately and can be more easily mis-interpreted. In light of his preceding description of the false teachers, Peter might be suggesting here that texts that deal with the ethical implications of Christian liberty (2:19) or the return of Jesus Christ (3:4) are difficult to understand unless, as New Testament scholar Richard Bauckham suggests, "they are interpreted in the light of the rest of Paul's teaching and of the apostolic teaching generally."[8]

Human Limitation and Error

The second reason relates to our finite and fallen human nature. As human beings, we are subject to many limitations. In 2 Peter 3:16, Peter describes the false teachers as "ignorant" (NIV) or "untaught" (NASB). As just noted, they may have lacked the necessary framework for understanding Paul's specific teachings or simply been unskilled interpreters. In interpreting Scripture, ignorance is definitely *not* bliss! Instead, it can be the source of interpretive distortion. Careful instruction regarding how to interpret the Bible and how to access essential background information for the Bible may prevent many interpretive missteps.

Interpreters also may misinterpret a text because they devote too little time and effort to studying it or because they focus only on some of the details of the text while overlooking others. The interpreters and their followers that Peter has in mind may be prone to misreadings due to a superficial grasp of the Christian faith and its demands. This may be Peter's point in describing these individuals as "unstable," or spiritually and morally weak, in 2:14 and 3:16.

More problematic are those interpreters who intentionally mis-interpret a text. Assuming that Peter is referring to the same individu-als in 3:17, where he warns his readers to beware of "the error of the lawless," their "distorting" (3:16) of the text does not appear to be so innocent or harmless. Peter further describes their faulty interpretive practices as habitual ("as they do the other Scriptures"). Their motiva-tion in doing so is unclear, but if these individuals are the false teachers described in 2 Peter 2, they are deliberately spreading false teaching in order to justify their own misguided convictions and self-indulgent, ungodly lifestyles and to greedily exploit naive believers. Not all willful misinterpretation will have a negative impact on an entire Christian community. Some interpreters consciously or unconsciously impose an unlikely meaning on a text in order to blunt its painful or offensive message so that they will not be convicted of their sinful behavior or troubled by the implications of its theological claims. Others may seek too eagerly for "biblical" affirmation of their personal views, standards, and beliefs. Similarly, ministry leaders may seek "biblical" support or a scriptural slogan for a new program they are launching. Finally, there are other interpreters who have a bias against the supernatural and therefore reinterpret biblical prophecies and miracle accounts in order to remove all divine involvement from the process.

Poor Training

The third reason why readers misinterpret biblical texts relates to their faulty spiritual conditioning. In other words, they have been trained to do so! It is not clear that Peter has this reason in mind in 2 Peter 3:14–16. However, the false teachers, as described in 2 Peter 2:21, "have known the way of righteousness" only to later "turn their backs on the sacred command that was passed on to them," although we do not know who or what led them to do so. Apparently they also are seducing others, who may have been within the community of faith, to embrace their teachings and take this radical step away from their Savior (2:14). In fact, Peter's opponents in 2 Peter may have been recognized as teachers by the churches, which would account for Peter's stern warnings. Most Christians are inclined to imitate the interpretive practices of those whom they respect as their spiritual mentors and teachers, both in the local church and through Christian print, broadcast, and electronic media. If they are regularly exposed to sloppy hermeneutics, it is not surprising if their own interpretive work is also flawed.

A related, widespread problem is an incorrect view of the Spirit's work. Citing a verse like John 16:13, which assures Jesus's disciples that the Spirit of truth "will guide you into all the truth," they confidently assume that proper biblical interpretation is a by-product of the Holy Spirit's indwelling presence. Accordingly, there is no need to receive any instruction regarding proper interpretive practice, nor any danger of misinterpretation. (We will explain why this viewpoint is incorrect in the next chapter.) And, finally, seduced by the extreme pragmatism that pervades modern Western cultures, Bible readers, like the Prayer of Jabez fan club, are often inclined to believe that whatever sounds good, works well, and sells briskly must be correct.

These claims that I have derived from 2 Peter 3 may strike you as extreme and unjustified, perhaps even as arrogantly harsh and self-righteously critical. However, the following summary of 2 Peter 3:14–16 by Richard Bauckham sounds alarmingly similar to our contemporary situation:

> For all their pretensions to be teachers, they have never bothered to acquire sufficient knowledge of Christian teaching to be able to understand either Paul or the other Scriptures which they also misinterpret. . . . Whatever their misinterpretations of Paul and of the "other scriptures" were, they used them to justify immorality.[9]

Stick with me for another chapter as I seek to defend the claim that interpreting the Bible is a difficult, demanding, and spiritually dangerous task. This flows directly from the Christian confession of Scripture as both a divine book and a human book and from a proper understanding of how God "speaks" to us today through Scripture.

In the concluding chapter I will offer a detailed explanation of why it is so important to interpret and apply the Bible correctly. In the meantime, however, consider the following: we don't like it when someone (e.g., one of our children) misquotes or misinterprets something we have said, wrongly deriving from our words permission to do something or support for their viewpoint. This is even more upsetting when that child in the process skews what we intended to communicate. For the same reason, we should be careful to use Scripture in ways that respect the biblical author's intentions. (In this case, there is no basis for concluding that the author of 1 Chronicles wanted us to pray Jabez's prayer repeatedly.) Otherwise we are merely misappropriating biblical authority to support our own ideas.

Think about It

1. How should we evaluate conflicting claims regarding the accuracy of Bruce Wilkinson's interpretation and application of the prayer of Jabez? What role should the record sales of his book and the positive testimonies of individuals who have prayed this prayer play in such a debate?
2. Consider the prayer in Genesis 24:12–14, which God answered in a remarkable way. Is this a prayer that we should pray today, especially if we are looking for a spouse? If so, how much of the prayer is a model for us? Why?

3. Have you encountered false teachers similar to those described by the apostle Peter in 2 Peter 3:14–16? How did you determine that their teachings involved a distortion of Scripture?

Read about It

1. Robert Stein, *Playing by the Rules: A Basic Guide to Interpreting the Bible* (Grand Rapids: Baker, 1995). Stein, a seminary professor, compares biblical interpretation with a sport or game that only works if you follow the rules.
2. D. A. Carson, *Exegetical Fallacies*, 2nd ed. (Grand Rapids: Baker, 1996). A prominent New Testament scholar claims that even Bible "professionals" (including himself) can make mistakes in interpreting the Bible.
3. James W. Sire, *Scripture Twisting: 20 Ways the Cults Misread the Bible* (Downers Grove, IL: InterVarsity, 1980). Sire, a senior editor, examines many of the ways in which false teachers rely on misinterpretation of the Bible to bolster their beliefs.

2

The Roots of Faulty Interpretation

Examining Our Convictions about Scripture

"It seemed good to the Holy Spirit and to us. . . ."

Acts 15:28

Back in 1974, during a national conference for religion professors, I saw a man passing out free materials. Not wanting to miss out on a "bargain," I hurried over and got a copy for myself. What was he distributing? A self-published, personally autographed book entitled *I Have Found an Elephant in the Bible*. My first impression as I skimmed through this 130-page work was that this author was playing a joke (and a rather expensive one) on the hundreds of stuffy scholars who eagerly grabbed his book. But as I read his introductory comments, it became clear that he was very serious about his interpretive conclusions. Examining the description of the *behemot* (the Hebrew word for "beastly beast") in Job 40:15, which he takes to be an elephant, he asserts with confidence that "Behemoth and JESUS CHRIST are the one and same thing" (or, the elephant symbolizes Jesus). After all, both Behemoth and Jesus spent time in the Jordan

River (Job 40:23; Matt. 3:13) and both are "first among the works of God" (Job 40:19; compare Col. 1:15). Thus his study of the elephant in the Bible offers "the key that will unlock the Hebrew Scriptures and give us a complete picture of JESUS CHRIST."[1] This man's book presents a rather unusual expression of a conviction that is widespread within the Christian church, namely, that Jesus Christ is the subject and center of the entire Bible and not just of the New Testament. Many Christians thus seek to "find" him on virtually every page of the Bible—even in the description of the *behemot*!

A second conviction commonly held by Christians is stated briefly and absolutely by David Barton: "There is no issue that the Bible doesn't address" (referring in context to the capital gains tax).[2] In other words, since the Bible is the Christian's operating manual for life, God must have packed it chock-full with everything we need to inform all of our attitudes and actions. There is a comparable theological claim that is usually labeled the "sufficiency" of Scripture, but Barton's conviction is not necessarily based on any specific biblical texts. For centuries, Christians have been known as "people of the Book," a description that expresses how important the Bible is for them in everyday life. Sometimes, however, total, unquestioning reliance on its words is coupled with a tendency to cite them unreflectively. This can lead to serious confusion and misuse when it is not grounded in an accurate understanding of the nature and proper interpretation of Scripture.

A third conviction about Scripture is less problematic but requires further discussion: the Bible is both a divine *and* a human book. For many theologians, this has prompted a comparison with the two natures of Jesus Christ. Just as Jesus was fully human and fully divine, so Scripture is both completely human and completely divine in origin. To be sure, this analogy has its limitations. For example, even if an error were to be discovered in the Bible, that would not have the same moral weight as a sin committed by Jesus. But it may help us to grasp some essential characteristics of the Bible.

Throughout the centuries the church has been forced to combat unbalanced understandings of the relationship between Jesus's two natures. These heresies emphasized one nature at the expense of the other, for example, claiming that Jesus only *seemed* to be human (or divine) but did not really bear that nature. Similarly, over the course of the centuries, the pendulum has swung back and forth regarding how Scripture should be viewed. Some have so emphasized its divine origin that the human authors are reduced to the Holy Spirit's "pen."

Others focus so much attention on the human authors that God's involvement is even denied or reduced to a creedal affirmation that they don't really believe. In their opinion, the human authors wrote about God, but God did not contribute directly to the actual writing process.

Neither one-sided emphasis does justice to passages such as 2 Peter 1:20–21 and 3:15–16. The former claims that prophetic Scripture did not originate in human interpretive efforts but resulted from the Holy Spirit's initiative. Therefore, the prophetic authors truly "spoke from God." The latter passage affirms the apostle Paul's dependence on divinely granted wisdom in writing his epistles. (It also notes that his various writings are theologically consistent.) This is not the place for a full exploration—or defense—of the nature of Scripture as a divine and human book.[3] Our goal here is rather to consider the implications of this doctrine for how we *interpret* the Bible since how we *view* what we are interpreting greatly affects how we *read* it. Consider how differently we read a love letter than a phone book!

Reading the Bible as a Divine Book—Like No Other

Theologically speaking, the Bible is the uniquely inspired Word of God. In both its origin and its perfection it is distinct from all other "religious" books, no matter how devout and inspiring their authors are. As a result, it displays a number of significant features.

First of all, the Bible has a unique Spirit-produced unity. This is not to deny the remarkable diversity found in the Bible. After all, the Bible resulted from many different *authors* at different *times* and in different *places* employing different *styles* and different *literary forms* to address different *audiences* with different *concerns*. For example, the style and contents of Proverbs and 1 Corinthians are quite diverse, but both arguably promote the same sexual ethic.

All of these writings together form a sacred anthology—the "canon," that is, the theological norm or standard for the community of believers. All of its books bear testimony to the one God, who is both our Creator and the Father of our Lord and Savior Jesus Christ. Despite various emphases in the individual books, we can expect there to be a shared coherent message running through the Bible from beginning to end. This message reveals God's unfolding "rescue plan" for humanity. And if the Holy Spirit guided the human authors of the Bible, then we should expect the Bible to be consistent. Therefore, we may legitimately seek to resolve or harmonize apparent conflicts. We may also expect to find numerous interconnections between books as later authors allude to earlier events in Israelite history, cite authoritative writings, and reuse prior traditions. Some of these interconnections involve a biblical author announcing that an earlier prophecy has now been fulfilled because God, according to Scripture, is able both to predict the future and then to bring it about (Isa. 44:26; 45:21).

Second, the contents of the Bible are unique. Although the Bible shares some features with other ancient texts, it is unique both in its claims and in its scope (covering all of human history from the original creation to the new heavens and new earth). It also makes unparalleled assertions about its own authority and truthfulness. Some believe that God does not intervene in human affairs (thus holding to a "closed universe"), or they simply view the Bible as an influential but exclusively human book. Such people may reject the Bible's claims to reveal God's true nature and to recount (sometimes miraculous) divine involvement in human history.

In seeking to explain, summarize, and apply the teachings of Scripture, all Christian literature may share some common goals of inviting and nurturing faith. Scripture, however, possesses a unique spiritual value and capacity to change lives. But this, in turn, requires that anyone who reads the Bible must be able to understand its basic message. Furthermore, understanding must be followed by application. The interpretation of any text that does not lead to a personal engagement with its message is incomplete.

It is because so many Christians share these convictions about the Bible that they instinctively turn to it to explain their actions and decisions and, more formally, to defend their policies and programs. In whatever they say and do, they want to be "biblical." And if they pay close attention to how others use Scripture, they soon discover, much to their surprise and delight, that there is a handy verse for every occasion—yes, "for every activity under the heavens" (Eccles. 3:1). But that is precisely the reason why we must consider the implications of reading the Bible as a human book.

Reading the Bible as a Human Book—Like Every Other

Despite its "heavenly" message, the Bible shares many features with most other books and therefore must be read in a similar manner. For example, it uses normal human language. As recently as the nineteenth century, it was widely held that New Testament Greek was a unique "Holy Ghost" language. But it was then demonstrated that the New Testament authors simply used the everyday language of the people. Although not many ancient Hebrew texts from outside the Bible have been found, it is clear that they use words and grammatical structures similar to those of the Old Testament. It is the contents of the Bible that are "holy"—not the language.

Most Christians, however, can't read Greek or Hebrew. As a result, the Bible is the most translated book ever written. It is a fundamental conviction of Christianity that the teachings of Scripture must be accessible for every believer to read rather than just for the elite religious leaders. This conviction drove people like John Wycliffe to bravely face persecution and death on the eve of the Protestant Reformation in order to make the Bible available in the common language. The fact that we generally read the Bible in translation has two main implications for interpretation.

First, since there is no perfect correspondence in words or grammar between the biblical languages and any modern language, every translation represents a compromise between clarity and conformity to the original. This makes it necessary to consult more than one translation of a biblical text in order to become more aware of interpretive options and nuances in meaning that we would miss if relying on only one translation—regardless of which one.

Second, since divine truths are communicated in *our* language in our translated Bibles, the better we understand our own language, the more clearly we will hear God's message. That might require us to review the basic grammar categories, such as verb tenses, the function of conjunctions (linking words such as "although," "but," "since," "unless"), and the difference between adverbs and adjectives. Furthermore, as we seek to understand the basic building blocks of communication, we need to be aware that a single word can have a wide range of meanings. These meanings develop over time and are determined by how the word is used in a specific context (this is known as *semantics*).[4]

As biblical scholars began to discover and translate a growing number of texts from the ancient Near Eastern world in the third to first millennia BC and the Mediterranean world of the first century AD, they realized that the biblical authors frequently use the literary forms and conventions of their contemporaries. Some Old Testament laws and proverbs are virtually identical to Mesopotamian or Egyptian versions. And New Testament letters contain the same basic features as the everyday correspondence in secular society. Comparing parallel genres from the biblical world and noting how they have been adapted to serve *divine* purposes can give us valuable insights into how the timeless message was communicated in culturally relevant ways.

These considerations all point to a crucial fact that we sometimes forget when reading the Bible: the timeless words of God were written by human authors in time and space.[5] Since biblical authors could assume that their readers had a sufficient knowledge of their own history and culture, they did not need to explain related details when mentioning them in their writings. We, however, need to learn as much as we can about biblical times, lest we read our own cultural and historical understanding into biblical texts. Furthermore, we have no indication that the biblical authors took dictation from God. Therefore, we should expect that their writings will reflect their individual personalities and unique uses of language rather than exhibiting a uniformity of style and content. The resulting diversity in the Bible presents us with an interpretive challenge as we seek to reconcile apparently contradictory claims and to discover theological unity. But this is a legitimate undertaking, given our conviction that the whole Bible was inspired by the Holy Spirit, as discussed above.

Finally, we must affirm that God communicates with us through the way human language normally functions, that is, through the plain sense of the text. To be sure, some biblical texts use everyday situations to express profound spiritual truths (for example, the parables of Jesus in Matthew 13). Others use vivid descriptions of blaring trumpets and unearthly beasts to paint a metaphorical portrait of future events without explaining exactly how they will unfold (Rev. 9). In both cases, the authors usually signal how they intend their words to be taken. Normally, no effort should be made to look for a hidden or mystical sense *behind* the clear words of Scripture. That, however, does not keep new individuals from claiming every few years to have discovered the interpretive key that unlocks the mysteries of God's Word. Such "Bible code" crackers even argue that this hidden key provides evidence that the Bible is, in fact, divinely inspired.[6] I received an unsolicited email earlier this summer from someone who concludes, after decades of study, that Psalm 128:3 offers undeniable proof that the divine Trinity includes a *mother*. (Read the text for yourself and see if you are convinced!)

God wants to speak directly to people today without requiring them to find 3D reading glasses or join the inner circle of some all-knowing teacher. In many cases, this means that we need to *unlearn* some bad reading habits so that we can read the Bible the way we read other texts, like one of Shakespeare's comedies, for example. Some parts of the Bible may require more effort on our part, and footnotes explaining unfamiliar expressions may be helpful. But we *can* understand the Bible on our own. That is one of the convictions underlying this book.

Cloning Balaam's Donkey—Strange Ways God Allegedly Speaks Today

I have to admit it—Numbers 22 is a strange text! According to the author of Numbers, "The LORD opened the donkey's mouth" so that it could complain to Balaam about being beaten. And without any hesitation, "Balaam answered the donkey" (vv. 28–29). I don't know whether the donkey's or Balaam's speech is more surprising. In any case, the donkey had more insight into the true state of affairs (that is, who was in charge of blessing and cursing) than did either Balaam or Balak, king of Moab.

Recently I have heard some even stranger claims regarding how God speaks to us today, especially through Scripture. We have already mentioned the first one—the claim that the Hebrew text of the Old Testament contains hidden messages, including the name of the Austrian emperor Franz Joseph I and the cure for diabetes, as well as predictions of the assassination of Egyptian president Anwar Sadat, the rise of the Iraqi leader Saddam Hussein, the date of his first attack using Russian scud missiles, and the opposition of US General Schwarzkopf. These can be discovered by means of ELS (equidistant letter sequences), which involves repeatedly skipping the same number of letters before writing down the next letter (for example, selecting every fiftieth letter) and then discovering words in the sequence of letters thus isolated.[7] It is relatively easy to find a specific word in the Hebrew text, for example, "scud." But we must ask how this type of "word search" for the predictive voice of God relates to the primary purpose of the Bible, which is not to warn Israel about a modern-day enemy rocket attack but to reveal the redemptive covenantal plan of God for delivering his people from the consequences of their sinful rebellion through the work of the Messiah.

A second questionable way in which God allegedly speaks is when a person randomly selects a Bible verse and takes it as God's specific guidance. A man prays for God's direction for overseas missionary service and, while reading the book of Isaiah, lands on Isaiah 18:2—"Go, swift messengers, to a people tall and smooth-skinned, to a people feared far and wide, an aggressive nation of strange speech, whose land is divided by rivers." This must be God's guidance, he concludes, but he may or may not end up going to the Ethiopians, the people to whom the verse refers (ancient Cush). At the same time, a woman is trying to decide whether to give an unexpected ten-thousand-dollar inheritance to her local church or build a family room. Also reading Isaiah, Isaiah 54:2 catches her eye—"Enlarge your house; build an addition. Spread out your home, and spare no expense!" (NLT). "That was easy!" she exclaims. Now I would not presume to know all the ways God can work in the world, but if these are good examples of how God speaks to us today, then he could use the *Chicago Tribune* or the *AT&T Real Yellow Pages* just as easily as the Bible to do so. (By this method you could speed up the process by closing your eyes, letting the Bible fall open, placing your finger randomly on the page, and claiming whatever it touches as a word from God just for you.)

A third strange approach involves sweeping through the Scriptures from Genesis to Revelation and identifying every verse that contains a promise as God's personal word of blessing on our life. New Testament scholar Scot McKnight calls these "sanctified morsels of truth." He describes this practice as taking "random verses, with blessing on top of blessing or promise on top of promise."[8] To be sure, some of these promises clearly apply to us today, such as 2 Peter 1:3—"His divine power has given us everything we need for a godly life through our knowledge of him who called us by his own glory and goodness." But the same cannot be said of Mark 14:13—"Go into the city, and a man carrying a jar of water will meet you."

A fourth approach turns all of Scripture, especially the storylike historical narratives, into marching orders for Christians today. "In this story God is telling me directly how I should think, act, and speak since the Bible is God's inspired Word." Accordingly, a wife treats her husband like Abigail treated Nabal because the Bible says to do so: "Please pay no attention, my lord, to that wicked man Nabal. He is just like his name—his name means Fool, and folly goes with him" (1 Sam. 25:25). And a husband demands that his wife call him "her lord" (1 Pet. 3:6). Such an approach, however, can lead to a reader confusing *sinful* or downright *stupid* actions recorded in the Bible with divine instructions.

We already mentioned a fifth approach, finding Jesus under every textual leaf, in our discussion of the book *I Have Found an Elephant in the Bible* at the beginning of this chapter. This approach is experiencing growing support today and is based on the twin convictions that (1) Jesus is the central theme of the Bible and (2) all of Scripture points to him. The former is true to a degree, although Old Testament scholar Gerhard Hasel is probably more accurate in declaring that "God is the center of the OT as its central subject."[9] The second conviction is based on an overinterpretation of Luke 24:27—"And beginning with Moses and all the Prophets, he [Jesus] explained to them what was said in all the Scriptures concerning himself." This led a pastor to declare in a sermon I heard recently, "If you don't find Jesus on the page of Scripture you are reading, keep reading it until you find him there."

This goes well beyond finding Jesus in predictive prophecy; it turns all Old Testament texts into predictions of or, more precisely, pictures foreshadowing the coming of Jesus. Accordingly, in Numbers 11:8 ("The people went around gathering it [the manna], and then ground it in a hand mill or crushed it in a mortar. They cooked it in a pot or made it into loaves. And it tasted like something made with olive oil"), the manna represents Jesus. After all, John 6:33–35, 48 teaches that he is the Bread of Life. Moreover, the grinding, crushing, and cooking in Numbers 11:8 represent Jesus's sufferings on our behalf. But what does the olive oil taste represent in the case of Jesus? And how did the people gather him up? The book of Hebrews and other New Testament texts give a warrant for some degree of christological (that is, Christ-centered) interpretation of Old Testament texts. This is usually called *typology* (see chapter 5 for further explanation). But there appear to be no limits on the creative and speculative interpretation to which this can lead.

What exactly does Luke 24:27 claim? A similar verse later in the same chapter may help to clarify the point Jesus was making: "Everything must be fulfilled that is written about me in the Law of Moses, the Prophets and the Psalms" (Luke 24:44). Jesus points here to the scope of the Old Testament's anticipation of the Messiah's coming: all three major subdivisions of the Hebrew canon look forward to him. In Jesus's postresurrection Bible study, he was not asserting that *every* biblical text is "about" or "pointing to" him. Instead, he was explaining to his disciples those passages throughout the Scriptures that spoke of him in order to clarify the world-altering nature of the prior week's events.

The sixth and final approach that we will mention here is the most difficult to deal with: a person simply tells the rest of his Bible study group that the Holy Spirit revealed to him what the text means or how we are supposed to apply it to ourselves today. How can we argue with God, even if a close reading of the text suggests that this interpretation is unlikely to be correct?

How the Holy Spirit "Turns on the Light"

This final approach—an individual claiming a direct revelation from the Holy Spirit—is quite common in the church today. It rests on the claim that God has promised in the Bible that he will guide us in all our spiritual interpretive work in such a manner that we cannot go wrong. He will show us the true meaning of each text regardless of how much or how little we heed the principles of sound interpretation or consult the interpretive work of godly biblical scholars. A textbook on biblical interpretation relates the following incident:

> One seminary professor tells how a crying student once interrupted a seminar on principles for understanding the Bible. Fearful that he might have offended the student, the teacher asked if anything was wrong.
> Sobbing, the student responded, "I am crying because I feel so sorry for you." "Why do you feel sorry for me?" The professor was perplexed. "Because," said the student, "it is so hard for you to understand the Bible. I just read it and God shows me the meaning."[10]

This viewpoint probably stems from a faulty interpretation of John 16:13—"But when he, the Spirit of truth, comes, he will guide you into all the truth." John 14:26, part of Jesus's same teaching session, helps to clarify the nature of the Spirit's guidance: "But the Advocate, the Holy Spirit, whom the Father will send in my name, will teach you all things and will remind you of everything I have said to you." In this address to his disciples given just hours before being betrayed and crucified, Jesus refers repeatedly to his "teaching" (vv. 23, 24). Therefore, he is probably speaking narrowly of the role the Holy Spirit will play in safeguarding the disciples' weighty responsibility to accurately preserve the Gospel records of the ministry and teaching of Jesus. In that case, he is not describing the ongoing ministry of the

Spirit in the lives of individual believers. According to John 15:26, however, the Spirit's task is to testify about Jesus, and he can clearly do this for believers today as well. The Spirit confirms the truthfulness of Jesus's claims and teachings in our hearts so that we are willing to commit ourselves to believing and obeying them.

This ministry of the Holy Spirit is commonly referred to as *illumination*. But there is some disagreement among Christians regarding *how* he shines light on the biblical text, or more specifically, what effect this illumination has on the interpreter. Theologian Millard Erickson emphasizes that the "Holy Spirit's role is not to convey new information that is not in the biblical text but to give insight or deeper understanding of the meaning that is in the biblical text."[11] He then goes on to explain in more detail what this involves, lest his words be understood as supporting the sixth approach noted above:

> It is not opposed to the careful study of the text. In a sense, the Holy Spirit is able to work more effectively, the more objective knowledge one gains of the meaning of the vocabulary and syntax of the text, for he works through the information, not independently of it. His work is more like that of tutor than of a lecturer.[12]

The Beginning and End of Faulty Interpretation

These strange claims about how God speaks today through Scripture lead to misinterpretation and misapplication. If I am correct that such problems are widespread in the church and in popular Christian publications today, when did this practice begin? Some would claim that the New Testament authors were the first culprits. Speaking of the use of the Old Testament in the New Testament, Old Testament scholar Peter Enns writes: "It seems to run counter to the instinct that context and authorial intention are the basis for sound interpretation" and is "unappealing . . . for *our* eyes." Enns goes on to claim that the New Testament authors, though "commenting on what the [Old Testament] text actually *meant*," made no effort "to remain consistent with the original context and intention of the Old Testament author." Instead, they sought to explain what the Old Testament "means *in light of Christ's coming*"—and so should we.[13]

Enns's conclusions concerning the New Testament use of the Old Testament are not shared by all.[14] Admittedly, some of the New Testament texts do use the Old Testament in puzzling ways. An example of this is 1 Corinthians 10:2–4—"They were all baptized into Moses in the cloud and in the sea. They all ate the same spiritual food and drank the same spiritual drink; for they drank from the spiritual rock that accompanied them, and that rock was Christ." Paul refers here to several well-known events following Israel's departure from Egypt: the cloud that guided and protected them (Exod. 13:21–22; 14:19–20), the crossing of the sea on dry land (Exod. 14:21–22), and the miraculous provision of manna and water in the wilderness (Exod. 16:35; 17:6). His claims regarding Moses and Christ, however, are unexpected. Most of the time, though, the New Testament authors use the Old Testament in a straightforward manner, as in the quotation of Proverbs 3:11–12 in Hebrews 12:5–6—"And have you completely forgotten this word of encouragement that addresses you as a father addresses his son? It says, 'My son, do not make light of the Lord's discipline, and do not lose heart when he rebukes you, because the Lord disciplines the one he loves, and he chastens everyone he accepts as his son.'"

Other scholars might trace faulty interpretation—or interpretation that is overly creative and speculative but edifying—back to the early Jewish and Christian interpreters. The early Jewish interpreter Philo of Alexandria (ca. 20 BC–AD 50) explored the significance of the Israelite dietary law that declared "clean" those animals that have divided hooves and chew the cud (Lev. 11:1–8, 26; Deut. 14:3–8). He suggested that "both these signs are symbols of the methods of teaching and learning most conducive to knowledge." Cud chewing thus represents the student "repeating in his memory through constant exercises" that which he has been taught, while the divided hoof represents the twofold path of life with the call to turn away from vice and stick to the path of virtue.[15]

About two centuries later, also in Alexandria, the Christian interpreter Origen offered the following explanation of the parable of the Good Samaritan from Luke 10:25–37:

> The man who was going down is Adam. Jerusalem is paradise, and Jericho is the world. The robbers are hostile powers. The priest is the Law, the Levite is the prophets, and the Samaritan is Christ. The wounds are disobedience, the beast is the Lord's body, the [inn], which accepts all who wish to enter, is the Church. . . . The manager of the [inn] is the head of the Church, to whom its care has been entrusted. And the fact that the Samaritan promises he will return represents the Savior's second coming.[16]

Allegorical interpretations such as these continued to flourish, developing in the Middle Ages into an emphasis on the "fourfold sense" of Scripture—(1) the literal or historical, (2) the allegorical or doctrinal, (3) the moral or ethical, and (4) the future or eschatological. In the Reformation period, however, this approach was brought into question. As Luther put it, "allegory is like a beautiful harlot" whom "idle men" in particular find irresistible.[17]

Now by no means did all early interpreters abandon an interest in the literal meaning of the biblical text, nor did the Reformers completely distance themselves from spiritualizing approaches. Theologian David Steinmetz suggests that the three nonliteral senses correspond to the Christian virtues of faith, love, and hope.[18] In other words, in seeking the "fourfold sense" of Scripture, highly trained interpreters attended to the literal meaning of each text, while also guaranteeing that it addressed the interpreter's world and fulfilled its God-given purpose to be "useful for teaching, rebuking, correcting and training in righteousness, so that the servant of God may be thoroughly equipped for every good work" (2 Tim. 3:16–17).[19]

As we look back on how the Bible has been interpreted in the past, it should provide us with both a warning and a challenge. On the one hand, the drive to edify the church through scriptural interpretation, which continues unabated up to the present, does not justify every hermeneutical somersault undertaken in order to achieve this end. On the other hand, the learned allegorizing commentaries of prominent medieval interpreters often have little in common with small group Bible studies in which everyone does what is right in their own eyes. The purpose of this present book is not simply to decry the excesses of contemporary interpretive efforts. It seeks also to encourage us to imitate the best efforts of previous generations of Christian interpreters. We too should use the Bible to address our own questions concerning who we are, what we should believe, and how we should live as the people of God, while paying careful attention to the original context and meaning of these ancient, divinely inspired texts.

Think about It

1. How do you understand the Holy Spirit's role in helping you understand the Bible? Can you cite any biblical support for your position? How would you respond to a friend who claims that

God told her what a specific verse means when you strongly disagree with her interpretation?

2. How should we evaluate the allegorizing interpretations of earlier (or contemporary) interpreters, such as Origen's explanation of the parable of the Good Samaritan cited above? Is it acceptable as long as it is spiritually edifying and not contrary to sound theology? Can we conclude that the Holy Spirit led him to interpret the text in this manner?

Read about It

1. Jacques Berlinerblau, *Thumpin' It: The Use and Abuse of the Bible in Today's Presidential Politics* (Louisville: Westminster John Knox, 2008) offers many fascinating—and exasperating—examples of how political candidates misuse the Bible in an effort to win votes.

2. In *Three Views of the New Testament Use of the Old Testament*, edited by K. Berding and J. Lunde (Grand Rapids: Zondervan, 2008), biblical scholars Walter C. Kaiser Jr., Darrell L. Bock, and Peter Enns present, illustrate, and defend their view and critique the views of the other two contributors.

3. Moisés Silva, in *Has the Church Misread the Bible? The History of Interpretation in the Light of Current Issues* (Grand Rapids: Zondervan, 1987), and Henry Wansbrough, in *The Use and Abuse of the Bible: A Brief History of Biblical Interpretation* (London: T & T Clark, 2010), offer a focused survey of the history of biblical interpretation.

3

The Consequences of Ignoring Context

Cartoonists exploit it, campaigning politicians complain about it, and, unfortunately, many Christians regularly engage in it. People commonly use familiar phrases or sayings in a manner that is contrary to their original meaning, sometimes doing so intentionally. We call this practice "taking the words out of context."

A few humorous examples will illustrate the matter. In a *Mother Goose and Grimm* cartoon, Mother Goose, on the phone, apologizes to her pastor: "Sorry Reverend, I'll have to miss the church social today. . . . I can't leave all my children." In the next panel we see the television announcer's words: "And now back to 'All My Children'" (the soap opera). Depending on its context, the phrase "all my children" could refer to two very different things! In the cartoon *Shoe*, a reporter, sent to cover the "big speech," notes the senator's promise, "And, in conclusion, I offer a hopeful vision of what lies ahead." The resulting article bears the headline "Lies Ahead," which the reporter defends as "a direct quote."

A college-age couple is saying good-bye before heading in opposite directions for the summer. The young man gives his girlfriend a card on which he has written out Genesis 31:49: "May the LORD watch between you and me when we are absent one from the other" (NASB).

He intends it as a sentimental—and impressively pious—expression of his affection for her along with his desire that God will preserve their relationship until they reunite in the fall. She, however, has taken an Old Testament survey course and understands the original context of these words. Laban, after pursuing Jacob for a week, angrily accuses him of sneaking off with his daughters and grandchildren "like captives in war" (v. 26) and stealing his household gods, before receiving Jacob's blistering counteraccusation of how Laban consistently cheated him for two long decades. Verse 49 aptly sums up the only thing to do in such a situation: "Since I don't trust you and you don't trust me, I solemnly call upon the all-seeing God to keep a vigilant eye upon you to make certain that you don't mistreat my daughters!" (Perhaps this is a fitting verse to write on a Hallmark card after all, given the lure of summer romances.)

The preceding examples indicate that "context" can be understood in several different ways—referring, for example, (1) to Mother Goose's personal situation, (2) to the content of the senator's speech, and (3) to specific events in the life of Jacob, as narrated in the book of Genesis. When interpreting the Bible (or any other written text, for that matter), the word "context" most often refers to the flow of thought in a passage, for example, how a specific sentence is related to the sentences that precede and follow it. We know that an individual word, such as "key" can refer to more than one thing (for example, a piano key or a small Florida island), depending on the sentence in which it is used. The same is often true of a sequence of words, such as "He changed the *key*." (Was he a musician or a locksmith?) Since this sentence can bear more than one meaning, the surrounding sentences help determine which meaning is correct when it appears in a specific paragraph. And when we ignore the surrounding paragraph, we are in danger of taking the sentence "out of context."

The Problem of Prooftexting

In dealing with the Bible, our conviction that the Bible is the Word of God and, consequently, that its specific contents are the very words of God may result in a dangerous practice. This involves treating individual verses of Scripture or even brief phrases as independent divine declarations that retain their meaning and authority even when removed from their literary context. The practice is usually labeled "prooftexting," leading to the warning that "a text without a context is a pretext for a proof text."[1] The term "proof text" has not always had a negative connotation, often being used to describe earlier systematic theologians' practice of listing biblical passages from which they derived Christian doctrines.[2] More recently, however, the term "proof text" usually refers to the arbitrary use of isolated Bible verses to support anything a person wishes to defend or promote—from lifestyle choices to new church programs—regardless of whether the text originally referred to anything remotely related. Although such use may not undermine sound doctrine, it nevertheless misappropriates biblical authority.

The way in which some versions of the Bible are printed actually facilitates this practice. The ancient manuscripts of the Bible lacked verse numbers; these were not added to the Greek New Testament until the mid-sixteenth century. When the King James Version was published, it indented each verse, and some modern translations, such as the New American Standard Bible (1963 ed.) followed this practice. This gives the reader the false impression that each verse constitutes an independent paragraph. In fact, in some cases, single sentences in the KJV span more than one verse (for example, Exod. 20:5–6; Matt. 5:21–22, 23–24; Eph. 1:3–6; Phil. 1:3–7), despite the fact that each verse begins with a capital letter.

Four Types of Biblical Context

Citing mere snippets of a biblical text and thereby ignoring its literary context is arguably the most frequent source of misinterpretation. This is complicated by the fact that there are at least four aspects of context that can be distinguished when discussing the Bible.

Literary Context

The *literary* context is the text surrounding an individual verse or passage. This may be visualized as a set of concentric circles beginning with the sentences that immediately precede and follow the verse in the middle, moving outward to the paragraph, the chapter (or complete textual unit), the subsection of the biblical book, the biblical book, and so forth. Each of these "circles" may have some bearing on the meaning of an individual verse. Paying attention to context is thus comparable to working on a jigsaw puzzle—the significance of an individual puzzle piece is not primarily determined by its shape or its combination of colors but by the complete picture of which it forms a part. Similarly, the meaning of a given verse is not exclusively determined by the words it contains and their interrelationships but rather by the immediate and larger context that surrounds it. Ignoring the literary context can lead interpreters to misunderstand and therefore misuse a text.

In the following paragraphs, I will discuss a number of examples taken from popular Christian books in which the author has misinterpreted a biblical text as a result of paying insufficient attention to its context. I will also note in each case how paying more attention to context will redirect the interpretation and application of the text. I am not assuming that the authors of these examples (and of other examples throughout the book) are deliberately misinterpreting the Bible. To the contrary, in many cases they are not even seeking to interpret the text; instead, they are merely using the text to make or support a point that is important to them. To the extent that this point, however, is not based on a correct interpretation of the text, they are misusing it—and in the process modeling deficient hermeneutics that need to be corrected. I view my role here like that of an athletic coach who reviews the game-day films with the team so that they can see what went wrong in the past before showing them how to play better the next time. Accordingly, I will also cite examples of the proper use of specific texts.

In their book *Boundaries*, Henry Cloud and John Townsend understand the phrase "'Come now, and let us reason together,' says the LORD" in Isaiah 1:18 (NASB) as indicating that God, "like a real friend, or a real father," wants to hear our side of things and will consider changing his mind.[3] The larger context of Isaiah 1, however, indicates that the addressees are so wicked that they can be described as "people of Gomorrah" (v. 10; see Gen. 18:20–19:25), whose worship is rejected by God (vv. 11–15) due to their "evil deeds" (vv. 16–17). God already knows their side of the story only too well; his indictment of Israel for blatant sin is irrefutable and the "guilty" verdict is already certain. Thus God's call here to "reason together" challenges the people to listen to reason as he sets before them the only two options open to them: repentance resulting in forgiveness or continued rebellion leading to destruction (vv. 19–20).

Christian interpreters love to use biblical phrases to reinforce their claims. For example, after lauding Joseph's "heroism" in marrying his pregnant fiancée, Mary, John Eldredge calls on all men to come to the rescue of "a beauty" (that is, a damsel in distress), citing Isaiah 61:3: "They will be called oaks of righteousness." He employs this quotation to portray how, "under the shadow of a man's strength, a woman finds rest."[4] Isaiah 61, instead, offers a comforting promise of reversal, restoration, and renewal and perhaps even a messianic prophecy of the work of Jesus Christ. (Note Jesus's intentional reading of this text in the Nazareth synagogue and explanation of it as being fulfilled in him, recorded in Luke 4:16–21.) Contrary to Eldredge's use, the Isaiah passage is not a description of "manly men" but of the future transformed state of "those who grieve in Zion"—presumably including both men and women. The remainder of the verse confirms that this is not a portrait of those who realize their masculine calling but a redemptive work of God intended to glorify *God* rather than men who fight for their woman: "They will be called oaks of righteousness, a planting of the LORD for the display of his splendor."

Anne Ortlund similarly mines the Scriptures to portray "biblical womanhood." In a chapter titled "Your Public Life," she encourages women: "You represent Christ. Hold your head up, as Psalm 3:3 tells you to." She even clarifies what she has in mind here: "Plan your shampoos so that you don't go to the grocery store in rollers. Switch purses—it's worth the time—so that you coordinate when you go out."[5] And what exactly does Psalm 3:3 tell us to do? Nothing! It simply acknowledges who God is: "But you, LORD, are a shield around me, my glory, the One who lifts my head high." The original psalm has nothing to do with grooming or color-coordinated accessories. Psalm 3's historical title associates it with David's flight after his son Absalom's successful coup (2 Sam. 15). Hotly pursued by enemies who taunt him that God will not deliver him (vv. 1–2), David nevertheless calls out to God, confident that he will deliver him as his shield, his (source of) glory, and the one who *lifts heads* (vv. 3–4). In its historical context, the latter phrase may refer to God's sovereign restoration of the shamed king (2 Sam. 15:30) to royal honor. This is a divine action, not a call to the "beautiful woman" to optimize her public appearance and then confidently lift her own head. By ignoring the literary context, Ortlund has turned a faith-filled prayer into a warrant for heading to the beautician!

In calling for people to experience mystical, supernatural Christianity today, John Crowder points to the account of the rebuilding of the temple under Zerubbabel's leadership in Zechariah 4 as an example of what we should expect. "But it is time we begin to look at the great miraculous works of the saints merely as blueprints for what is available to every believer. Blueprints for the latter house of God's glory, which will shine with unprecedented brilliance. As in Zechariah 4, the Lord's hand has laid the foundation of that house, 'His hand will also complete it.'"[6] There is a problem with Crowder's claim, however. He has both ignored the context in Zechariah 4 and misquoted the verse. According to verse 9, "The hands of Zerubbabel have laid the foundation of this temple; his hands will also complete it." In other words, the "hands" referred to here are Zerubbabel's, not God's (see also v. 7). To be sure, this task was accomplished, "'Not by might nor by power, but by my Spirit,' says the LORD Almighty" (v. 6), but the reconstruction of the temple was not a "miraculous" deed by any normal understanding of this term.

In light of how frequently popular interpreters (or users) of Scripture ignore the literary context and misinterpret texts as a result, someone might get the impression that determining the context of a verse and its implications for understanding that verse is a difficult task. It is true that some biblical texts, such as the prophetic books, may be more difficult to analyze, and it is unclear exactly how the individual laws or proverbs are arranged within their respective collections. But even in studying these literary genres it is helpful to examine the verses that surround a specific text. In most texts, however, it is no more difficult to determine the flow of thought than it is in a news or topical magazine, in personal correspondence, or in a legal document.

Take Philippians 4:13, for example: "I can do all things through Him who strengthens me" (NASB, similarly ESV). To determine what the "everything" Paul refers to here involves—rather than simply assuming that the scope is global, ranging from passing algebra, to climbing Mount Everest, to securing a date with the captain of the cheerleading squad—we simply need to examine the verses that immediately precede and follow this verse.[7] The preceding verse suggests that Paul is speaking primarily of "being content in any and every situation, whether well fed or hungry, whether living in plenty or in want" (v. 12), confident that God will provide for his needs (see also vv. 11, 16, 19). Thus this verse, understood within its literary context, is appropriately applied to difficult situations in which we find ourselves as a result of our obedience toward and ministry for Jesus.

There are also Bible study tools available that can assist us in the task of understanding context. Most study Bibles and one-volume commentaries break down chapters into logical subsections, also indicating when a text continues on into the next chapter. This is not to suggest that the implications of a verse's context are always clear or undisputed. Matthew 18:20 ("For where two or three gather in my name, there am I with them") is frequently cited with regard to Christ's presence at our prayer gatherings, and some commentators agree with this use. Most commentators, however, note the phrase "two or three witnesses" a few verses earlier (v. 16) in setting forth the proper procedure for church discipline.[8] (In verse 16 Jesus draws on the requirement for the corroborating testimony of two or three witnesses in an ancient Israelite criminal trial; see Deut. 17:6; 19:16–17.) This suggests that verse 20 may conclude a section on church discipline rather than referring specifically to prayer. Jesus is assuring the disciples that when they carry out church discipline "in his name"—as difficult as this may be—he is also "present" during the process and, thus, his authority is delegated to them. Therefore, whatever they "bind on earth will be bound in heaven" (Matt. 18:18). In any case, the literary context gives us no warrant for universalizing the promise, as Dan Montgomery does: "Being a Christian does not mean that you no longer feel afraid. . . . The good news is that the Holy Spirit and other Christians are with you, calming your fears and easing your burdens. In our very midst is Jesus himself, strengthening us through the radiance of his wholeness."[9] This may, in fact, be true, but not on the basis of this verse's promise when rightly understood *in its literary context.*

Historical-Cultural Context

Even though the Bible contains universal truths, which pertain to Christians around the world and throughout the centuries, its books describe ancient events and were initially addressed to specific readers who lived two to three thousand years ago (or even earlier). Contemporary authors can assume that their readers today are aware of many features of popular culture—the latest electronic gadgets, the names of successful sports teams, recent movies, and hit songs—and therefore do not need to explain them when mentioning these in writing. Similarly, biblical authors wrote with a particular readership in mind, who shared a common knowledge of key events in Israelite history, religious practices and core theological beliefs, as well as of Israelite cultural practices and values and, probably to some degree, those of neighboring peoples. Accordingly, any of these can be mentioned without explanation. But the Bible reader today, often lacking such knowledge, may not understand these cultural features and may wrongly equate aspects or practices of modern culture—whether regarding slaves or salads, banquets or boots, weddings or warfare—with those described in the Bible.

For example, Larry Crabb, in discussing communication in marriage, turns to Ezekiel 24 to help gain "a biblical perspective" on "how God looks at feelings."[10] In this chapter God announces to the prophet Ezekiel the imminent death of his beloved wife and, at the same time, forbids him from carrying out the customary mourning rituals (vv. 16–17): "Yet do not lament or weep or shed any tears. Groan quietly; do not mourn for the dead. Keep your turban fastened and your sandals on your feet; do not cover your mustache and beard or eat the customary food of mourners." How unexpected it must have been to receive such instructions! Crabb fails to mention that similar mourning practices are described positively elsewhere in the Old Testament as well as in other ancient Near Eastern documents. The mourning rituals Ezekiel is commanded not to perform were normal accepted practices in ancient Israel: loud wailing (Jer. 9:17–18), sprinkling dust on an uncovered head (Job 2:12), removing sandals (2 Sam. 15:30), covering the face (Mic. 3:7), and eating a funeral meal (Jer. 16:7). In fact, in Jeremiah 9:17–18 God calls the people to summon professional mourners in light of Jerusalem's impending doom. Such expressions of honor for the deceased need to be understood in their ancient context before comparing them with modern practices like sending flowers to the funeral home and visiting with the close relatives in the presence of an open casket.

Therefore, it is clear that God is not giving Ezekiel normative instructions about the proper way for Israelites to mourn in the future but rather specific instructions limited to a particular situation. As God explains, Ezekiel's odd actions are to serve as a sign-act that anticipates the even greater imminent loss of the temple in Jerusalem, which the Babylonian army would destroy (Ezek. 24:20–24). Despite noting "the special prophetic circumstances of Ezekiel's experience," Crabb nevertheless proceeds to derive "a very helpful principle from God's command to 'groan quietly.'" We are to "subordinate the public expression of our feelings to the goal of allowing God to use us for His purposes."[11] It is questionable whether God was seeking through this incident to teach us (or even Ezekiel) how to express our feelings properly in public, especially given the development of extensive mourning rites in both the ancient and modern worlds, quite unlike other common human emotions. More likely, the text is illustrating how completely God took over the lives of his chosen servants, the prophets, making their lives a part of their message. And, if we are committed to carrying out his will in our lives and serving his kingdom purposes, we may similarly expect some unexpected, or even difficult, assignments.

A common approach to biblical narratives is to retell them in a contemporizing, interpretive fashion by both substituting modern cultural features for the ancient description and emphasizing the basic story line rather than the textual details. John and Stasi Eldredge do this with the story of Ruth: "Ruth takes a bubble bath and puts on a knockout dress," and while Boaz is "drunk," Ruth uses "all she is as a woman to . . . arouse, inspire, energize . . . seduce him."[12] Although it is not uncommon for interpreters to conclude that Ruth and Boaz went even further, having sex that night on the threshing floor,[13] this behavior is completely contrary to the character of Naomi, Ruth, and Boaz as presented throughout the book. Furthermore, the Hebrew word *simlah* used in Ruth 3:3 designates the common unisex outer garment that could double as a blanket when sleeping outside and hardly "a knockout dress," so the ESV's "cloak" is more accurate than the NIV's and NASB's "best clothes" (Ruth 3:3).

More problematic, however, is the way in which the Eldredges ignore the chapter's historical-cultural setting. The issue here is the need for the foreign widow Ruth to obtain protection and financial provision, which her mother-in-law Naomi cannot supply. It is not about sex, and there is nothing seductive or sexually arousing about exposing a man's lower limbs to the night chill and quietly lying down at his feet. When Boaz awakens, Ruth immediately makes her cause known: "Spread the corner of your garment over me, since you are a guardian-redeemer of our family" (3:9). She is calling for a symbolic gesture that indicates a personal commitment (compare Ezek. 16:8) from one who has a social obligation to care for her rather than offering an invitation to "dive under the sheets" together! According to the Eldredges, however, "This is seduction pure and simple—and God holds it up for all women to follow when He not only gives Ruth her own book in the Bible but also names her in the genealogy."[14]

The other Old Testament book named after a woman, Esther, is also given a questionable interpretation in a devotional by James and

Shirley Dobson. In their view, there is no "better example of honor between husband and wife than the biblical account of Queen Esther and Xerxes, king of Persia." We should emulate this behavior, "approaching each other as husband and wife with the deep respect and honor we would show royalty," since it will result in "a home environment that is more loving, positive, and enjoyable than you ever thought possible."[15] The Dobsons carefully note Esther's various expressions of honor—waiting patiently in the king's hall, touching his scepter, inviting him to two consecutive banquets, and using phrases such as, "If the king regards me with favor and if it pleases the king" (Esther 5:8).

Although the Dobsons as interpreters are aware of the Persian court protocols that extend even to members of the royal harem, they fail to acknowledge that Esther's behavior is thus that of a *subject* seeking to approach the *king*, not that of a *wife* appropriately honoring her *husband* because of the inherent value of such conduct. And there is no indication in the book that the marriage of Esther and Xerxes prospered as a result of her deferential behavior—but she did survive her unscheduled meeting with the king and save her people. Perhaps the biblical text is intended rather to illustrate how to avoid getting executed by your partner if he is a powerful and impulsive person!

Every biblical text reflects in some respects the times in which it was written. One guide to biblical interpretation lists the following aspects of historical-cultural background: worldview; societal structures; physical features; economic structures; political climate; behavior patterns, dress, or customs; and religious practices, power centers, convictions, rituals, or affiliations,[16] and this list could be expanded. Not every text depends on the knowledge of such background information for proper interpretation, but in many cases this knowledge will enhance our understanding of the text. For example, when Paul refers to being led "as captives in Christ's triumphal procession" (2 Cor. 2:14), a knowledge of the Roman imperial post-battle victory parades will help to clarify his use of the word "captives" here and prevent us from quickly equating this with a typical American Independence Day parade today. The exact cultural background that is assumed by an author may not always be apparent. In 2 Corinthians 2:14–16, the word "aroma" is commonly associated with incense that is spread along the streets during such a procession, but it may, in fact, be an independent (Old Testament) image related to God-pleasing sacrifices. In any case, it is helpful to read the notes of a good study

Bible or consult a more detailed reference work (see the Read about It section at the end of this chapter) if we get the sense that a biblical text is describing a world that is foreign to us and thus that we are in need of some additional information.

There can be a danger, however, in giving too much weight to a text's proposed historical-cultural context. Since this background is usually implicit rather than explicit—that is, *presupposed* by the author and *reconstructed* by the interpreter—it can be problematic to take it as the key factor in determining meaning. Rob Bell, for example, has championed in several publications the importance of understanding the relationship between a first-century rabbi and his disciples in interpreting the Gospel narratives. His reading of various identified and unidentified sources, some of which are from the second century or later, lead him to make some novel interpretive claims, which may or may not be warranted.

For example, Bell explains the account of Peter walking on the Sea of Galilee, as recorded in Matthew 14:22–34, as follows: "If you are a disciple, you have committed your entire life to being like your rabbi. If you see your rabbi walk on water, what do you immediately want to do? Walk on water." Peter's problem, then, when he begins to sink is that he "loses faith in himself . . . that he can do what his rabbi is doing." After all, Jesus as rabbi chose Peter and the other disciples primarily on the basis of their great potential.[17] Yet since the text does not clearly indicate what motivated Peter to attempt to do what Jesus did—or whether his actions here are foolhardy or exemplary—it is questionable whether one should supply the motivation from a claimed knowledge of rabbi/disciple dynamics. And, in light of other Gospel narratives about faith and doubt, it is more likely that the faith Peter lacked was not "in himself" but in the unlimited power of God that was present in the person of Jesus (compare Matt. 8:24–26).

Salvation-Historical Context

The Bible not only contains hundreds of individual stories of people carrying out or opposing God's purposes in this world. It also offers one extensive "story" (today sometimes called a "macronarrative"), which stretches from the creation to the consummation of human history as we know it, climaxing in the creation of a new heavens and new earth. This story has sometimes been presented as a drama consisting of several acts, with believers today participating in the last scene before the opening of the final act.[18] Over the course of this lengthy history, God has progressively revealed himself and his plan to his people and further developed his way of relating to them. Foundational to this plan and relationship are the various covenants (or contract-like agreements) that God has made with Israel and the church. As a result, it is important to determine at what point in this grand story a particular text is located. Otherwise, we may be inclined to misread an earlier text by interpreting it in light of later developments.

Jay Adams does this with Numbers 14. According to this text, after hearing the scouting report of the twelve spies concerning the Promised Land occupied by the Canaanites, the Israelites decide that it would be better to return to slavery in Egypt than to proceed. This provokes God's judgment. Writing on the subject of divine forgiveness, Adams claims that forgiven sinners are never subsequently *punished* by God, even though their sins may have continuing consequences that nevertheless always serve a beneficial purpose. Thus God's word of judgment condemning the rebellious exodus generation to die in the wilderness without entering the "Promised Land" must be understood not as a punishment but as ultimately for the benefit of the church. In support of his claim, Adams cites 1 Corinthians 10 (more specifically v. 6: "Now these things occurred as examples to keep us from setting our hearts on evil things as they did"), a text that explicitly refers to the rebellion narratives recorded in Exodus and Numbers.[19]

To be sure, the history of God's people was recorded and preserved in the Bible so that we can learn from their acts of both faith and disobedience. But this does not change the fact that Israelites dying in the wilderness were being punished by God, as 1 Corinthians 10:5 indicates: "Nevertheless, God was not pleased with most of them; their bodies were scattered in the wilderness." It would be of little comfort for any of them to be told by Paul that later believers would benefit from their failure! What the narratives of Exodus and Numbers make clear is that, following the ratification of the Israelite (or Sinai) covenant in Exodus 19–24, every rebellion results in the punishment (and frequently death) of some Israelites. Since the Israelites' rejection of the Promised Land is the fourth and climactic rebellion (out of seven recorded in Numbers), their punishment is certain, despite their subsequent confession of guilt (Num. 14:40). Although Moses's intercessory prayer results in forgiveness (vv. 20–23), their punishment is merely lessened (from the total destruction of the nation to the deaths of that generation), not completely avoided.

Psalm 51:11 offers another vivid example of the danger of ignoring the salvation-historical context. In the midst of a prayer of personal lament, this verse records the following plea of David: "Do not cast me from your presence or take your Holy Spirit from me." Is this a request that a Christian today should pray? Is there any New Testament text that suggests that God's Spirit could be removed from us contrary to our heart's desire? The New Testament speaks of grieving (Eph. 4:30) or quenching (1 Thess. 5:19) the Holy Spirit but not of driving the Spirit out of our lives. This makes it likely that Psalm 51:11 may be an exclusively "BC" prayer, which is limited to the period of salvation history when God's Spirit temporarily equipped God's special servants (that is, judges, kings, prophets, priests) for a specific task rather than indwelling and empowering all believers.

The psalm title associates this psalm with David's acts of adultery and murder involving Bathsheba and her husband Uriah (2 Sam. 11–12). If this is the historical setting, then David may have had Saul's demise in mind. Because of Saul's repeated disobedience, the Spirit departed from Saul and came upon David instead (1 Sam. 16:13–14). In addition, Saul was permanently denied any further prophetic guidance (1 Sam. 15:35; 28:6). Therefore, we need not fear, like David, that God might remove his Spirit from our lives.[20] This is not to suggest, however, that Psalm 51 does not offer us an appropriate example of how to confess our sins before God, pleading for his forgiveness and restoration, but we will probably not conclude our similar prayers with "May it please you to prosper Zion, to build up the walls of Jerusalem" (Ps. 51:18) either.

Theological-Thematic Context

A novel does not normally consist merely of a series of chapters that develop the plot and characters. It usually also develops a theme or message through the telling of the story, such as the importance of courage and determination in facing adversity or the consequences of evil deeds. Nonfiction works can also emphasize specific principles in the course of their chapters, and we can identify the development of thematic emphases within individual biblical books. Even though interpreters may not agree on the primary message or emphasis of a book, they usually agree on its dominant theological themes, such as "holiness" in Leviticus, "seeking the LORD" and "divine retribution" in Chronicles, "belief/faith" in John, and "love" in 1 John. Individual texts, in turn, presuppose and contribute to these themes. This consti-tutes, so to speak, the text's theological-thematic context. Accordingly, when studying a text, it is helpful to identify its dominant themes and note how these themes are developed elsewhere in the book.

In their discussion of the causes of depression, Frank Minirth and Paul Meier quote Isaiah 43:8 ("Lead out those who have eyes but are blind"). They note how frequently the Bible (or God) refers to human blindness and conclude that "all of us humans have blind spots."[21] Who would dispute, from personal experience, that this is a true statement? Nevertheless, there is a big difference between "blind spots," such as a driver commonly experiences when a car passes on the right, and complete blindness, which is the metaphor commonly used in Scripture. Within the book of Isaiah, it becomes a dominant metaphor, along with hardened hearts and deaf ears, in characterizing the people's profound spiritual insensitivity and their future healing and restoration by God. The word "blind" occurs thirteen times in the NIV translation of Isaiah, while the Israelites' inability to "see" and related terms (for example, "closed/sealed eyes," "be sightless," "do not see") are mentioned around twenty times (see especially Isa. 42:7, 16, 18–19). The problem with Minirth and Meier's use of Isaiah 43:18 is twofold. First of all, by citing this verse in connection with their claim regarding blind spots, they imply that the book of Isaiah (and the Bible as a whole) teaches this, bestowing a "biblical" status on their observation of human nature. More significantly, their use of this verse completely misses the point of the metaphor, which emphasizes Israel's complete inability to carry out God's calling for them to be a servant nation, rather than merely suggesting some minor limitations.

In a section labeled "Ecological Reconciliation," Bernard Bangley makes the following "green" claim: "The Bible assures us, over and over again, that human life will be better, more prosperous and more enjoyable, when we take care of the natural resources God has given us in a responsible manner."[22] He cites Leviticus 26:3–5 to support this claim:

> If you follow my decrees and are careful to obey my commands, I will send you rain in its season, and the ground will yield its crops and the trees their fruit. Your threshing will continue until grape harvest and the grape harvest will continue until planting, and you will eat all the food you want and live in safety in your land.

This interpreter disregards the theological context of these verses and therefore misinterprets this text. The book of Leviticus can be subdivided into three major sections, each of which develops one aspect of God's demand for holiness: chapters 1–10, holiness in worship; chapters 11–24, holiness in everyday life; chapters 25–27, holiness in the Promised Land. Chapter 26 sets forth the future consequences—the blessings (vv. 3–13) or the curses (vv. 14–39)—of Israel's behavior in their new home, along with the possibility of restoration after exile and judgment on the basis of God's covenantal promises to Abraham, Isaac, and Jacob (vv. 40–45). Bangley thus has the order wrong here. It is not environmental stewardship that leads to prosperity and enjoyment in life. Rather, Israel's obedience to God, including avoiding idolatry and worshiping him properly (vv. 1–2), will be rewarded by an abundance of rain and bountiful harvests.[23] And since this text is directed to Israel as God's chosen covenantal people, it is also not clear that these promises and threats are directly transferable to any modern nations.

Isaiah 6 is often labeled "the call of Isaiah," although it is unclear that this marks the prophet's first encounter with God. (For example, the prophecies of Isaiah 2–5 may precede Isaiah 6 both *chronologically* and *literarily*.) In any case, this text attracts interpreters to equate their "missionary call" with that of Isaiah, including a comparison of the modest spiritual results of their ministries. And no doubt many a Sunday school superintendent has made use of Isaiah 6:8 when seeking to recruit additional children's workers: "Then I heard the voice of the Lord saying, 'Whom shall I send? And who will go for us?' And I said, 'Here am I. Send me!'"

What is clear, however, when we study the various call narratives in the Old Testament (such as Exod. 3; Judg. 6; Jer. 1; Ezek. 1–2; Amos 7) or other texts in which God reveals himself to individuals (including Gen. 17:1; 18:1; 26:2; Judg. 13), is that God's appearance is always unsought and unexpected. The repeated testimony of the Old Testament is that God can break into an individual's life whenever and wherever he pleases, such as in a burning bush (Exod. 3), a winepress (Judg. 6), or a gentle whisper near the mouth of a mountain cave (1 Kings 19). God calls the prophets to their ministry and sometimes, as in the case of Moses and Gideon, he must drag them "kicking and screaming" into his service; they do not seek him!

Tommy Tenney, however, turns this biblical pattern on its head. He understands this text as offering guidelines on how to become a "God catcher" and "experience the manifest presence of God."[24] According to Tenney, we, like Isaiah, can "catch God," who "is very careful to hide so that He *can* be found. He *wants* you to find Him"—especially if there is "*urgency*" in our cry and we do not seek to accommodate "two kings in our lives." And Tenney speculates that Isaiah's divine encounter in the temple took place then because he "was just coming back from King Uzziah's funeral." In other words, he went to the place where God was most likely to be found and when the timing was right.[25]

First of all, the king's funeral may not have been recent. The phrase "In the year that King Uzziah died" (Isa. 6:1) is simply a typical ancient Near Eastern dating formula that associates events with other major events that occurred in a year, such as a death, a foreign invasion, or an earthquake (Isa. 20:1; Amos 1:1). Therefore it is unclear that Isaiah was caught up in mourning at the time or that the *other* king had to be removed before God, the true King, could reveal himself to Isaiah. Second, the text does not suggest that Isaiah was urgently seeking God at the time of his encounter, even if he was in the temple. In fact, it is possible that Isaiah's vision of God's throne did not even occur in the temple—the text never claims that the prophet was there, only that he had a vision of God seated in the temple—or in his heavenly palace (since the Hebrew word used here can designate either). In Isaiah 6, an emphasis on "catching God" is less important theologically than the themes of God's exaltation (Isa. 2:11, 17; 5:16; 33:5, 10; 52:13; 57:15), holiness (Isaiah's favorite name for God, "the Holy One of Israel," occurs twenty-six times), and glory (the Hebrew word used in Isa. 6:3 occurs thirty-five more times in the book).

Sometimes interpreters invoke a theological theme in a misleading manner, especially when they ignore other aspects of context. Richard Young, in a book that examines the question *Is God a Vegetarian?* rightly observes "the long tradition of prophetic indictments against empty formalism in worship," usually involving animal sacrifices. In his discussion of the prophets, he commendably quotes Isaiah 22:13–14; 66:3; and Jeremiah 6:20, and he notes Isaiah 1:11–15; 29:13; Hosea 6:6; Amos 5:21–24; and Micah 6:6–8, although he makes no claim to be comprehensive.[26] Young, however, appears to misunderstand the relationship between fellowship offerings and the eating of meat, an aspect of these texts' historical-cultural context (Lev. 7; also Deut. 27:7). He claims that it "appears that the people had turned animal sacrifice into a pretext to slaughter animals and eat their flesh," citing Hosea 8:13 and 1 Samuel 2:12–17 as examples.[27] Hosea 8:13 offers no clear support to Young's claim, and in 1 Samuel 2 the situation is clearly different from Young's characterization. In the latter text, the people are portrayed as sincerely following the requirements of the law, while Eli's wicked sons blatantly disobey them—against the will of those bringing the sacrifices—in order to satisfy their sinful cravings.

Young interprets Isaiah 22:13–14 similarly: "Isaiah comments that there is no atonement for those who needlessly and irresponsibly slaughter animals merely to gorge on their flesh, for doing so was considered an unforgivable sin."[28] But let's examine these verses more closely: "But see, there is joy and revelry, slaughtering of cattle and killing of sheep, eating of meat and drinking of wine! 'Let us eat and drink,' you say, 'for tomorrow we die!' The LORD Almighty has revealed this in my hearing: 'Till your dying day this sin will not be atoned for,' says the Lord, the LORD Almighty." Young conveniently omits the part of the text which is the key to its meaning: "'Let us eat and drink,' you say, 'for tomorrow we die!'" (v. 13). Isaiah 22 warns of an imminent military invasion of Judah as an expression of divine judgment against God's disobedient people (vv. 5–7). The leaders respond by shoring up Jerusalem's defenses and securing the water supply rather than looking to God in repentance (vv. 8–11). Instead of mourning their impending doom (v. 12), they fatalistically indulge themselves with one final party (v. 13). Their unforgivable sin (v. 14) is not eating meat but rather their refusal to repent in light of the coming judgment of God, as announced by the prophet.

This example illustrates how various aspects of context work together as we seek to determine the meaning of a text. It is not as difficult as it seems! In order to determine the literary context, all we have to do is broaden the scope of our reading of biblical texts beyond the individual verse to the paragraph or chapter that contains it in order to determine what the text as a whole is about. In the process, not only can we usually avoid improper prooftexting, but we will also enjoy a fuller understanding and appreciation of Scripture. As we become familiar with the individual books of the Bible, the Bible's historical-cultural background, and its major theological themes and learn to use some basic reference works, we will also pay more attention to other aspects of context.

God's Word deserves to be read and interpreted at least as carefully as a contract!

Think about It

1. Do you think it is all right to use a biblical text in a way that is contrary to its literary context and original meaning if it is helpful to the church and not contrary to biblical teaching? Why do you think this?
2. Revelation 3:20 is frequently used in connection with personal evangelism. Examine the immediate context of this verse— Revelation 3:14–22. Which details in these verses might indicate that this is an improper application of this verse?
3. A Christian ministry that gives financial advice encourages all couples to have joint bank accounts, citing Genesis 2:24 in support. Do you think this is an example of improper prooftexting? Why or why not?

Read about It

1. Craig G. Bartholomew and Michael W. Goheen, in *The Drama of Scripture: Finding Our Place in the Biblical Story* (Grand Rapids: Baker, 2004), give an easy-to-read account of God's unfolding plan of salvation and our place within it.
2. Two biblical scholars, Craig S. Keener (*IVP Bible Background Commentary: New Testament*, 1993) and John H. Walton (*IVP Bible Background Commentary: Old Testament*, 2000), have prepared helpful reference works that illuminate the historical-cultural background of texts on a chapter-by-chapter basis.
3. Two reference works that summarize the major theological themes of the individual biblical books, as well as synthesizing the development of these themes over the course of the entire Bible, are T. Desmond Alexander and Brian S. Rosner, eds., *New Dictionary of Biblical Theology* (Downers Grove, IL: InterVarsity, 2000), and Walter A. Elwell, ed., *Evangelical Dictionary of Biblical Theology* (Grand Rapids: Baker, 1996). Elwell's work is also available free of charge on some websites.

4

Divine Truth Expressed in Human Words

Challenges with Language

"Stop fighting over words."
2 Timothy 2:14 NLT

Humpty Dumpty makes a much-cited claim regarding word meaning in Lewis Carroll's fictional tale, *Through the Looking-Glass*:

"When *I* use a word," Humpty Dumpty said, in rather a scornful tone, "it means just what I choose it to mean—neither more nor less."
"The question is," said Alice, "whether you *can* make words mean so many different things."
"The question is," said Humpty Dumpty, "which is to be master—that's all."
Alice was too much puzzled to say anything.[1]

Words are the basic building blocks of any text and are very adaptable building materials indeed! We can use a word literally—"I am writing a *book* about interpreting the Bible"—or figuratively, often in common expressions—"she can read you like a *book*" or "she threw the *book* at him" or even "he cooked the *books*." Expressions like the latter can often be confusing to nonnative speakers of a language. And there are other uses for the word "book," for example, as a verb—to *book* a hotel room or to *book* a petty thief. A *bookmaker*, in turn, can refer either to a publisher or to someone who takes bets at the racetrack.

In each of these cases, context is decisive. By studying the context we can usually determine what meaning the author intended. In that sense the author *is* master, but not in the way Humpty Dumpty suggests. The author cannot simply make a word "mean so many different things." Instead, she normally chooses among the conventional meanings a word has in a given language, unless she is intentionally playing with language or seeking to coin a new usage, such as referring to a book lover as a "bookie" or telling a person "I booked you" to inform him that she ordered the requested novels. In such cases, the word is often placed in quotation marks to inform the reader that it is being used in an unusual way.

In his second letter to his close friend Timothy, Paul instructs him to warn those under his spiritual care against "quarreling about words" (2 Tim. 2:14; compare 1 Tim. 6:4). It is not exactly clear what kind of arguments Paul has in mind here, but he describes them as both devoid of value and destructive. He also mentions them in the immediate context of "godless chatter" (2 Tim. 2:16) and false teaching (vv. 17–18) and in contrast to handling "the word of truth" correctly (v. 15). As one commentator explains it,

> It would . . . be mistaken to think either that Paul was forbidding careful attention to the meaning of words—either those of Scripture or those we ourselves use—or that Paul was saying that it is wrong to engage, even to argue, with these people (cf. 2:25). The allusion is to quarreling, quibbling, wrangling over words, seizing on texts without due attention to their proper context, engaging in polemics, reveling in novel interpretations and disputed points of teaching.[2]

To be sure, there has been much "quarreling about words" in Christian circles in recent years. There have been disputes regarding whether it is appropriate, for example, to add "and sisters" when Paul addresses Christian "brothers" in his letters, to make it clear to the reader that he is speaking to women in the local churches as well (see in the NIV Rom. 1:13; 7:1, 4; 8:12, 29; 10:1; 11:25; 12:1; 15:14, 30; 16:14, 17).

There have also been heated debates about the implications of male "headship" (1 Cor. 11:3; Eph. 5:23). Some interpreters dispute translators' use of the phrase "practicing homosexuality" in 1 Timothy 1:10 (see also 1 Cor. 6:9 TNIV), equating the behaviors that Paul harshly condemns with only certain homosexual practices. And others argue against the decision to use the word "servant" rather than "slave" to designate literal social (and figurative spiritual) relationships in the biblical world. As these examples indicate, the interpreter of the words of Scripture faces some difficult challenges.

Challenges in Understanding Words

Most interpreters read the Bible as a translated work. As a result, their understanding of Scripture is largely dependent on the prior interpretive decisions of translators. This is true for two reasons. First, translators must decide how closely their translation of a verse should conform to its actual wording and grammar in the original language (that is, Hebrew, Aramaic, or Greek) rather than using modern idiom to communicate as clearly as possible the meaning of the verse as a whole. There is no one-to-one correspondence between the vocabulary and grammar of any two languages (for example, between the various uses of the English word "key" and the closest Spanish equivalents). Therefore, translators must choose between using the same English word as often as possible to translate a given Greek word in the New Testament or using a variety of English words to more accurately express the precise nuance of that Greek word in a given context. As a result, Bible translation constantly involves compromises between faithfulness to the ancient text and clarity today.

For example, note how the Greek word *sarx* is normally translated in the NASB as "flesh" but is represented in several different ways in the NIV and NLT:

Text	NASB	NIV	NLT
Mark 14:38	flesh	flesh	body
John 17:2	flesh	people	everyone
Rom. 8:6	flesh	flesh	sinful nature
Rom. 11:14	fellow countrymen	own people	people of Israel
1 Cor. 1:26	flesh	human standards	the world's eyes

Text	NASB	NIV	NLT
1 Cor. 3:3	fleshly	worldly	sinful nature
Gal. 5:16	flesh	flesh	sinful nature
Eph. 5:29	flesh	body	body
1 Tim. 3:16	flesh	flesh	human body
1 Pet. 4:2	flesh	earthly lives	lives

In this case, a Bible reader using the NLT would be mistaken to assume that the word "sin" appears in Romans 8:6; 1 Corinthians 3:3; and Galatians 5:16.

Second, in many cases, translators must choose between multiple interpretive options that the specific wording of a verse can support. For example, in 1 Thessalonians 4:4, the NIV reads, "learn to control your own body" (similar to most modern translations), while the footnote lists two viable alternatives: "learn to live with your own wife" and "learn to acquire a wife"—two very different meanings! Every translation is an interpretation of the text, and possible alternative translations are not always noted. Thus we may interpret and apply a given text differently, depending on which version we are reading.

Many interpreters prefer to read Scripture in the King James translation (or Authorized Version)—still the bestselling Bible today after four hundred years. This presents the further challenge of outdated language, which may be misunderstood by modern readers—unless they like the writings of William Shakespeare! For example, the KJV advises readers in Philippians 4:6 to "be careful for nothing" rather than "Don't worry about anything" (HCSB, NLT). And 1 Thessalonians 4:15 (KJV) informs us that, at the future coming of the Lord, those who are still alive will not "prevent" those who are asleep (that is, the deceased; compare the NASB, NIV, NKJV: "precede").

Furthermore, some biblical words have specialized—cultural or theological—meanings that may not be clearly conveyed by modern English equivalents. For example, a "counselor" [Heb. yo'ets] in the biblical world normally served in the royal court, giving advice to the king concerning domestic or foreign policy (2 Sam. 15:12; Prov. 24:6). Modern interpreters, however, often equate this figure with the trained psychologist who helps people resolve their personal problems. For example, psychiatrists Frank Minirth and Paul Meier cite Proverbs 11:14 ("Where there is no guidance the people fall, but in abundance of counselors there is victory," NASB) as a biblical endorsement of professional Christian psychotherapists.[3] The NIV is less supportive of their use of the verse: "For lack of guidance a nation falls, but victory is won through many advisers." Although both the ancient high court official and the modern Christian counselor may share some traits and activities, it is misleading to equate the two.

Common Mistakes Made with Words

The preceding considerations and example suggest that it is easy for popular Christian writers to misuse biblical words. In his helpful guide, *Exegetical Fallacies*, D. A. Carson distinguishes sixteen "word-study fallacies."[4] In this chapter I will illustrate a smaller number of ways in which biblical words are commonly misinterpreted, offering slightly different labels.

Anachronism

Our preceding example regarding the word "counselor" illustrates *anachronism*. This involves reading a much later meaning into a word used in an earlier text and ignoring the word's significance within its context in the ancient world. Shirley Cook does this in *The Exodus Diet Plan*. Citing the phrase "the fat of my sacrifice" from Exodus 23:18 (KJV), she asks, "Why not offer my fat as a sacrifice to God?" She reflects on how precious her body fat is to her in light of the time, attention, and money ("spent on milk shakes, corn chips and double-decker burgers") she has devoted to accumulating it. (The ESV translation would support her use even better: "the fat of my feast"!) As she sacrifices her fat to God, just as Israel offered up the Passover sacrifice, she is confident that God will show her "how to burn off the excess calories that have added bulges and bumps that don't belong."[5]

Israel's sacrificial offerings were mandated by God, and the complete prohibition against eating the fat or "suet" of sacrificial animals is never explained as intended to improve the people's health—in fact, it is never explained at all. (Moreover, the ban presumably did not apply to game animals; see Lev. 3:16–17 and 7:24–26.) The fat portions of the sacrifices were not necessarily more precious to the Israelites; they were simply demanded by God. To equate our excess pounds with a portion of an animal sacrifice risks reading the modern obsession with being thin into the rationale behind ancient sacrifices.[6]

A common case of anachronism involves the parable regarding the "talents" in Matthew 25:14–30. The Greek word *talanton* originally designated a measure of weight and later came to mean an amount of money; it was rendered in various English translations simply as "talent." Still later, from this usage in the KJV, the meaning "ability" developed, but the Greek word *did not* have this meaning during the New Testament period. Nevertheless, this later meaning is often read into the parable in Matthew. A rather typical example of this is by Rob Reynolds, who quotes a staff member of the Christian Action Network commenting on Matthew 25: "In the parable, the only servant who was chastised was the one who had done nothing with his talent while his lord was away. . . . We all have some kind of ability or talent. For me it's politics. For others it may be medicine or counseling or pastoring. We have to determine what our talent is and how we can best use it to do God's work on earth."[7]

Another frequent example of anachronism involves the word "vision." Popular authors sometimes cite Proverbs 29:18, often in the KJV translation: "Where there is no vision, the people perish." Then they proceed to write about the importance of developing and pursuing a "vision" for your local church or parachurch ministry. If you read the entire verse in a contemporary translation, however, you will discover that this is prooftexting. Note the NLT: "When people do not accept divine guidance, they run wild. But whoever obeys the law is joyful." The key word here is "vision" [Heb. *chazon*], which in the Old Testament refers to divine revelation communicated to a prophet, as in Isaiah 1:1; Obadiah 1; Nahum 1:1.

Jentezen Franklin uses Habakkuk 2:2–4 (NKJV) to address the same topic. After recounting the "goals" for his church that God had fulfilled and exceeded (and also about his "dream" wife, children, and house), he uses this text to encourage readers to pursue their God-given "vision" or "dream":

> Then the LORD answered me and said:
> "Write the vision
> And make *it* plain on tablets,
> That he may run who reads it.
> For the vision *is* yet for an appointed time;
> But at the end it will speak, and it will not lie.
> Though it tarries, wait for it;
> Because it will surely come,
> It will not tarry. . . .
> But the just shall live by his faith."

Franklin understands this text as giving "some very practical advice on how to handle" our personal vision—writing it down so we don't forget it and making it plain so we know where we're going.[8]

The Hebrew word for "vision" [*hazon*] is never used in the Old Testament to refer to God's plan for an individual's life, which the individual is consequently expected to relentlessly pursue—this is simply how the word is used today, especially in Christian circles. Instead, it normally refers in the Old Testament to God revealing in advance what he will bring about in a nation's future. The only exception to this exclusively nationalistic emphasis involves King David. "Vision" is used in 1 Chronicles 17:15 (ESV, NASB, NRSV) and Psalm 89:19 to refer to God's covenantal promise to bless David, the nation, and the nations, ultimately through his greatest descendant Jesus Christ. Yet even here, this was not a vision that depended on David's efforts in order for it to be realized.

The Root Fallacy

A second common misuse is called the root fallacy. This occurs when interpreters assume that the historical origin (or etymology) of a word determines its current usage. In such cases, they will often speak of the "original," "root," or "basic" meaning of the word. Etymology, unfortunately, usually has little to do with contextual meaning.[9] To call a person "nice" is not necessarily an insult, even though the word "nice" was originally derived from the Latin *nescius*, meaning "ignorant," and came down to us via a Middle English word meaning "strange, lazy, foolish." Similarly, to call a woman "homely" today is not a compliment, despite the fact that its original—and now obsolete—meaning is "domestic."

Robert Hicks devotes an entire book to presenting a biblical basis for identifying six stages of manhood.[10] He correlates these six stages with six Hebrew nouns used to refer to the male gender, grounding his argument on supposed "basic meanings" of these nouns derived from their etymologies: the creational male—*'adam*; the phallic male—*zakar*; the warrior—*gibbor*; the wounded male—*'enosh*; the mature man—*'ish*; and the sage—*zaken*. Hicks omits two additional common and equally relevant Hebrew "male" words (*ben* = son and, more importantly, *na'ar* = young man) without explanation. This may be because he only needs six words to correlate to the proposed six stages. More problematically, he explicitly claims that this is "what the Scripture has to contribute" to an understanding of the male life cycle.[11] In other words, God presumably revealed something noteworthy about "maleness" through the specific Hebrew words (and their etymologies) that refer to the male gender in the Old Testament.

Hebrew scholar James Barr warns against this "most damaging" practice "where etymological associations are allowed to do the work in interpretation that should be done by semantics [the study of word meaning] on the basis of actual usage."[12] A standard introduction to language and biblical interpretation decries the fact that "sermons, semi-popular writings, and even some more serious works, evince frequent examples of improbable conclusions drawn from etymologizing or from word-formation considerations."[13] One basic problem with Hicks's dependence on etymology is that Hebrew dictionaries are often uncertain about and thus in disagreement over a word's origin. Their suggestions are sometimes quite speculative and often depend on the claim that the origin and meaning of a Hebrew word are the same as that of a similar word in a related language such as Arabic.

For example, it is uncertain whether the noun *'enosh* was originally derived from a verb meaning "be weak, sickly"—on which Hicks bases his "wounded male" stage. Another standard Hebrew dictionary derives this word from a verb meaning "be friendly or social,"[14] in which case the author ought to suggest a different "divinely revealed" stage: *'enosh*—the well-connected man! But even if the former etymology is correct, it is simply incorrect to assume that the Old Testament uses the word *'enosh* whenever it wants to emphasize a man's weakness, or *'ish*, often better translated "person," to emphasize his maturity. In fact, *'enosh* is used in its Aramaic form in Daniel 7:13 to designate "one like a son of man, coming with the clouds," who is given authority over the eternal kingdom of God—hardly a picture of weakness! Given the arbitrary and dynamic nature of human languages, it is even less likely that these various words refer to distinct stages in the journey that every male must take. But this does not keep Hicks from expanding a faulty word study approach into a detailed chart of masculinity in the following manner:[15]

Enosh:

Summary idea: wounded warrior

Orientation: pain, hurt, grief, depression

Initiation rituals: significant loss, defeat, failure, divorce, disease

Unique needs: permission to grieve, articulate pain

Role of mentor: grants permission, offers insight on pain

Image symbol: open wound, blood

Biblical character: Job, Jacob

Contemporary illustrations: Jim Bakker, Vietnam vets, Iran Contra indictees

Application of faith: seeing God in the wound, accepting a purpose for the pain

Example of Jesus: Gethsemene, humiliation, crucifixion, rejection, Luke 22–23

Unfortunately, there is little biblical basis for his claims.

The root fallacy also surfaces when writers seek to exploit the "original meaning" of English words. For example, Anne Ortlund says the following about raising "enthusiastic" children: "That's how you want them to grow up. The word comes from *en Theo*, or 'in God.' Support them with words of faith, hope, and love, and in that framework—'in God'—they'll be ready to tackle anything."[16] Now Anne Ortlund may be offering sound advice to Christian parents, but it is sound *not* because of any etymological relationship between "enthusiasm" and God. (Indeed, the word's "original" meaning is actually closer to "being inspired or possessed by a [pagan] deity.")[17]

Overloaded Meaning

A third way in which writers misuse biblical words is when they take a word that has a wide range of meanings in the Bible and read several of them into one text, thereby "overloading" its contextual meaning. Creflo Dollar Jr. does this with the Greek word *soteria*. This word can be used in the New Testament to designate a number of beneficial actions, including not only salvation through the forgiveness of sins (Luke 1:77), but also sustaining life through eating food (Acts 27:34), deliverance from prison (Phil. 1:19), and preservation from drowning (Heb. 11:7). The related verb *sozo* can also refer to healing from disease (Matt. 9:21–22) or disability (Mark 10:52) and to the exorcism of demons (Luke 8:36). Dollar correctly acknowledges this: "The Greek word for *salvation* is *soteria*, which means 'healing, safety, deliverance, preservation, the ministering of angels, and soundness.'" Next, however, he cites Romans 10:9–10 which says, "With the mouth confession is made unto *salvation*" (v. 10 NKJV), and wrongly concludes that "with your mouth you bring into being your healing, that with your mouth you bring safety and soundness to yourself. . . . There is a direct connection between your mouth and prosperity."[18]

What Dollar does then is read into Romans 10 all the various meanings that *soteria* can have in a variety of different biblical contexts. Romans 10:9–10, however, is clearly referring to salvation from our sins and from God's wrath (see the reference to "the righteousness that is by faith" in verse 6). Furthermore, it cannot be demonstrated that *soteria* in the New Testament ever refers to what Dollar describes as "total life prosperity," which includes financial prosperity. A basic rule of interpretation is that, when a word has a wide range of uses in the Bible, only one of them is present in a given text unless it is clear that the author is deliberately playing with multiple meanings.[19]

Appeal to Unknown or Unlikely Meanings[20]

An especially devious misuse of biblical words occurs when an interpreter claims a meaning for a Hebrew or Greek word that is invalid or unlikely and offers no real textual support. In most cases, however, the typical reader has no way of knowing that this claim is incorrect. For example, Robert Schuller states incorrectly that "if we go back to the original Greek and examine the word that was originally translated as 'meek,'" we discover that this "is really not a good translation." Although most contemporary translations still use "meek" or "gentle" to translate the Greek word *praus* in Matthew 5:5, Schuller nevertheless asserts that a "better modern translation of the verse might be, 'Blessed are the mighty, the emotionally stable, the educable, the kindhearted, for they shall inherit the earth.'"[21] Unfortunately, this is simply not true, as any dictionary of ancient Greek will confirm. As a primary example of what it looks like to live the kind of lifestyle commended in Matthew 5:5, Schuller describes Linda Down, a victim of cerebral palsy, who accomplished a "mighty" achievement by "running" the 1982 New York marathon on crutches. This example indicates just how distant his understanding of this trait is from Jesus's self-description as one who is "*gentle* and humble in heart" (Matt. 11:29: "gentle" here also translates Greek *praus*).

Gary Comstock also attributes to a biblical word a nuance that it did not obviously have in biblical times, possibly in order to validate his own viewpoint. The detailed description in 1 Samuel of the relationship between David and Jonathan is a favorite of proponents of "gay sex," who have often interpreted David's words upon his friend's death as indicating that these two men were involved in a homosexual relationship: "I grieve for you, Jonathan my brother; you were very dear to me. Your love for me was wonderful, more wonderful than that of women" (2 Sam. 1:26).[22] Comstock, accordingly, analyzes the word "covenant" in 1 Samuel 18:3 [Heb. *berit*], which states, "And Jonathan made a covenant with David because he loved him as himself." He argues that this is "a convenient form for saying something that could not be said another way" in ancient Israelite society, even suggesting that this narrative may have been the work of a gay writer whose "altering and coding of terms would have been heard by other gay men with a recognizing ear."[23]

There are several other examples in the Old Testament of covenant making between two powerful individuals (Gen. 21:27; 31:44), and here we must remember that David and Jonathan were not simply two random Israelites—David was the king's son-in-law, and Jonathan the heir to the throne. Furthermore, the covenant between David and Jonathan and its reaffirmations are mentioned repeatedly (1 Sam. 20:8, 16; 22:8; 23:18), and it is unclear why the word "covenant" in particular would be used to refer to a committed homosexual relationship. Although the number of references to the "love" between David and Jonathan is unique within the Old Testament, the same verb [Heb. *'aheb*] is also used in 1 Samuel to describe Saul's, his subjects', and his attendants' love for David (1 Sam. 16:21; 18:16, 22).

Confusion Regarding Synonyms

One useful feature of a language like English is the existence of a number of words related to the same topic. In some cases, they differ in the object that they refer to but all belong to the same general category. For example, the category of residential building includes house, hut, condominium, apartment, cabin, mansion, and palace. We know that they share certain features in common but we have little difficulty distinguishing between them. Other words are so closely related—such as "regret," "remorse," and "repentance"—that we call them synonyms. Yet we may still realize that such words are not completely interchangeable. For example, "regret" does not necessarily imply a desire for forgiveness in the way that "repentance" does. To cite another example, an "apology" is appropriate in strained relationships between two people, but we speak instead of "confession" when we acknowledge our sin against God. The availability of related words like these enables us to describe objects, actions, and emotions more precisely.

The same is true of the words used in the Bible. When we are studying a particular word in a biblical passage, it can be helpful to look at other related words to determine whether the word before us bears a specific nuance that the related words lack. This might suggest why the author used that particular word rather than one of the other options, but it may be impossible to be certain. In a book presenting biblical principles for losing weight, Frances Hunter draws a faulty conclusion regarding the various Hebrew words for "fat." Convinced that God was calling her to go on a Daniel fast,[24] Hunter was troubled to read in Daniel 1:15 that the young Israelites who were given only water and veggies (or an all-grain diet) were "fatter" (KJV, NKJV, NASB, ESV) after ten days than all the others in the king's court. She thought to herself: "Well, if you're going to go on a 'Daniel fast' with the idea in mind of losing weight, who wants to be fatter when you finish than you were at the start?"[25] (Actually, there is no clear indication in the Bible that *losing* weight should ever be a person's physical or spiritual goal.)

Hunter's solution begins by noting that there are "many different words or definitions in Hebrew for the word 'fat.'" One standard Bible concordance, for example, lists at least a dozen different Hebrew words that are translated as "fat" in the KJV.[26] But what about the Hebrew word *bari'*, which is used for "fat" in Daniel 1:15? She claims to have learned—from some unidentified source—that the particular Hebrew word for "fat" used here "means 'to be anointed, satisfied, rich or fertile.'" Thus she concludes that Daniel and friends were "not necessarily fatter in flesh, but more anointed by the Spirit of God."[27] This involves a further faulty approach to studying words. Hunter takes a specific meaning (that is, "anointed") that the word may have in one context and transfers it to another context where that meaning is unlikely. She then concludes that this is the precise nuance that the author had in mind in using this particular Hebrew word here rather than a near synonym.

More problematic in this case is the fact that I cannot find any published source that gives "anointed" as an acceptable meaning for Hebrew *bari'*. (It appears that Hunter mistakenly has the Hebrew synonym *shemen* in mind here, which the KJV translates as "anointing" *only in* Isaiah 10:27!) In fact, an identical phrase is used in Genesis 41:2 to describe the fat cows in Joseph's dream. Would Hunter view them as "Spirit-anointed" as well? A much simpler explanation, though less supportive of her dietary agenda, is to suggest that, contrary to expectation, Daniel and his friends were better nourished and healthier than their fellow courtiers-in-training.

A different misunderstanding of biblical synonyms is displayed by Michelle McKinney Hammond, who discusses the biblical concepts of "blessing" and "curse," defining the latter as "*God's disregard . . . that allows us to fail*" (italics original). Hammond then considers what Psalm 66:18 says about unanswered prayer: "If I regard wickedness [iniquity] in my heart, the Lord will not hear" (NASB). She assumes that such a serious consequence would not result from merely committing "your garden-variety sin." Therefore, she reasons, the Hebrew word used for "iniquity" here [Heb. *'awen*] must be "at least two steps" worse. In support of her surmise, she then cites Exodus 34:6–7 and Daniel 9:24, both of which use the word "iniquity" in conjunction with the synonyms "transgression" and "sin(s)."[28] Unfortunately, in these two texts, the English word "iniquity" translates an entirely different Hebrew word: *'awon.* (It looks similar to the word used in Psalm 66:18 but begins with the Hebrew letter *'ayin* rather than *'aleph.*)

In other words, Hammond is discussing the meaning of the English word "iniquity" rather than what the author of Psalm 66 means by using the Hebrew word *'awen*—or how the various Hebrew words for *sin* differ from one another. Incidentally, not all modern translations translate this particular word in Psalm 66:18 as "iniquity," further undercutting her argument. The HCSB uses "malice," while the NASB uses "wickedness" and the NIV and NLT have "sin." Hammond claims, on the basis of her analysis, that "sin" and "transgression" represent lesser "stages" of disobedience, in which "repentance is still readily in reach." This, however, is no longer the case "when iniquity sets in." Hammond explains: "Sin is when you aim for the mark (righteousness) and miss it; transgression is when you acknowledge the mark but choose to do your own thing anyway. . . . Iniquity occurs when you decide the mark is not real or doesn't apply to you. You set your own standards."[29] Since she offers no textual data in support of her claims, they are difficult to evaluate. The word *'awen* occurs most frequently in Job, Psalms, and Proverbs to designate evildoers whose deeds include "malicious verbal abuse," "social atrocities," and "idolatry."[30] But God calls them to repentance (Job 36:10; Isa. 55:7), and the author of Psalm 119 prays that God will not allow *'awen* to rule over him (v. 133), suggesting that "repentance is still readily in reach" even for these individuals.

As the preceding examples make clear, it is easy to impose meanings on the words of the Bible. Sometimes this results from not giving adequate attention to the relationship between modern translations and the underlying Hebrew, Aramaic, and Greek words. You might think that it is difficult or even impossible to avoid such mistakes without a thorough knowledge of the original languages of Scripture. But this is not the case since there are a number of inexpensive reference works that enable the interpreter to do accurate word studies in the original language. An exhaustive analytical concordance offers a complete listing of every occurrence of every significant word that is used in a specific translation of the Bible. Through the use of subheadings or numbers in the margin, this type of concordance indicates for each entry which word is used in the original language. For example, Robert Young's *Analytical Concordance to the Bible* clearly indicates that Psalm 66:18 uses a different Hebrew word for "iniquity" from Exodus 34:7 and Daniel 9:24. In fact, it lists eleven different Hebrew words and five different Greek words that are translated as "iniquity" *at least once* in the KJV. It also cites twenty-two additional verses in the Psalms that use the same Hebrew word for iniquity as Psalm 66:18 (*'awen*). With this tool, anyone could study in depth how this particular word is used in the Psalms, while knowing for certain that they are doing a Hebrew-based analysis. Several exhaustive concordances are available online for free, and there are also some other helpful web-based tools that provide the same information. (One of the best currently available is www.blueletterbible.com.)

Misunderstanding Figurative Expressions

One of the striking features of the Bible is its abundant use of figurative language, not only in its poetic but also in its prose texts. By using metaphors derived from everyday observations and experiences, biblical authors can communicate complex and abstract theological concepts more effectively. Note how "the LORD God is a sun and shield" (Ps. 84:11) is a more powerful statement about God's actions on our behalf than if the psalmist merely wrote, "God provides for and protects us." Unless we pay close attention to these figurative comparisons, however, we can miss the point that the author is making and misinterpret the text. This is especially the case when it involves an image that is used frequently throughout the Bible, such as the contrast between light and darkness.

In their book *Becoming a Contagious Christian*, Bill Hybels and Mark Mittelberg encourage all Christians to share the gospel message more effectively with people they meet in their everyday activities. Offering "a lesson from light," they suggest that the biblical metaphor of "light" can help us understand how to do this. The "biblical use of the term 'light,'" in their view, emphasizes "clearly and attractively presenting God's truth to others . . . [that is,] lucidly articulating the content of the gospel message."[31] This description fits very well in a book on personal evangelism, but it is unlikely that an image as commonplace and suggestive as light will have the same nuance each time it appears in Scripture. In Matthew 5:14, "You are the light of the world," which Hybels and Mittelberg cite in support of their claim, Jesus interprets the "light" as his disciples' "good deeds" (v. 16) rather than a verbal witness. Some verbal clarification of the gospel is probably necessary, however, if those who observe these good deeds are to "glorify your Father in heaven" (as the verse concludes).

Another text cited by the authors is 2 Corinthians 4:6: "For God . . . made his light shine in our hearts to give us the light of the knowledge of God's glory displayed in the face of Christ."[32] Here as well the emphasis is not on the skilled communication of the gospel by individual believers but on God's supernatural illumination of unbelieving hearts. This is made clear by the contrasting claim that the "god of this age has blinded the minds of unbelievers" (v. 4). Furthermore, in discussing the essentials of effective gospel communication, verse 2 emphasizes the *integrity* of the messenger rather than the *style* of the message. Whenever we identify a figurative expression in Scripture, we need to examine closely how it is used in a specific context rather than making general statements about what this image (always) references.

Our dependence on translations as general Bible readers can lead to a variety of faulty conclusions regarding the meaning of specific words. We can read the modern meanings of English words into biblical texts that understood these words in very different ways or give too much importance to the word's "original" meaning. We can wrongly conclude that the meaning a specific word has in another context is also present in the text we are reading. And we can be too inclined to believe whatever an author says a word means "in the Greek." Such errors can be reduced by developing the habit of consulting more than one Bible translation and by learning how to use an analytical concordance or web-based word study tool.

Think about It

1. Reflect on how our interpretation of the Bible is affected by our use of—and dependence on—English translations. How can we use the availability of numerous modern English translations to help us in the interpretive task?

2. A once-familiar gospel song celebrates the fact that "I've got a mansion just over the hilltop," based on the KJV translation of John 14:2: "In my Father's house are many mansions." Pastors have long used this promise to encourage their weary—and often poverty-stricken—church members. And one author suggests that "dull preachers" might be downgraded from a mansion dwelling "because their preaching was so lifeless and dreary"![33] R. Thomas Ashbrook, however, presumably uses the word "many" in this verse as a biblical basis for his book *Exploring the Seven Stages of Spiritual Growth*. This book discusses seven mansions or castles having the same "network of rooms" to explore, each of which represents a category of "our spiritual experience."[34] Compare the KJV translation of John 14:2 with a number of modern translations. Then look up the word "mansion" in an English dictionary and note how its meaning has developed over time, leading up to its current usage: "a large, imposing house; stately residence."[35] Do you think Jesus was describing either palatial dwellings or stages of spiritual growth to his disciples?

Read about It

1. To learn more about the challenges of translating the Bible and how these affect the interpretive task, read Gordon D. Fee and Mark L. Strauss, *How to Choose a Translation for All Its Worth: A Guide to Understanding and Using Bible Versions* (Grand Rapids: Zondervan, 2007).

2. Get your hands on a copy of an exhaustive analytical concordance. There is one available for nearly every modern English

translation. Look up a favorite New Testament verse in that translation and then look up some of its key words in the concordance. See if you can figure out how the concordance indicates which Greek word lies behind the corresponding English equivalent and identifies other passages that use the same Greek word.

3. William D. Mounce has prepared an inexpensive and easy-to-use dictionary of biblical words that is especially helpful in distinguishing between synonyms: *Mounce's Complete Expository Dictionary of Old and New Testament Words* (Grand Rapids: Zondervan, 2006).

4. The best resource for understanding biblical imagery is Leland Ryken, James C. Wilhoit, and Tremper Longman III, eds., *Dictionary of Biblical Imagery* (Downers Grove, IL: InterVarsity, 1998).

5

Understanding the Literary Menu

How Genre Influences Meaning

> "In the past God spoke . . . in various ways."
>
> Hebrews 1:1

O nce upon a time . . ." This is one of the most recognizable beginning phrases in all of literature. It tells us that what we are reading is fictional, a make-believe fairy tale that did not happen and perhaps could not have happened. We do not expect the text that follows to narrate an incident from the American Civil War or from the Bible, and we assume that it will conclude with the words "and they lived happily ever after." In other words, the introductory phrase serves as a literary signal that helps us identify what type (or genre) of literature we are reading. This, in turn, triggers specific expectations and interpretive strategies in us as readers.

The Bible—a Diverse Anthology

One of the great treasures and challenges of the Bible is the fact that it is actually a unique and remarkable anthology of various kinds of literature, even though it develops a unified story line. The author of the book of Hebrews affirms this: "In the past God spoke to our ancestors through the prophets at many times and in various ways" (Heb. 1:1). The Old Testament prophetic books contain call narratives, vision reports, complaints, accounts of confrontations with opponents, descriptions of symbolic actions, parables, allegories, prayers, sermonic instructions, hymns, disputations, confessions, and doxologies, in addition to the more common oracles of judgment and salvation regarding Israel and the foreign nations. Each of these forms serves to communicate God's message.

Old Testament scholar John Goldingay offers the following comparison between the Bible and modern literature:

> Imagine, then, "Gibbon's *Decline and Fall of the Roman Empire*, the collected poems of T. S. Eliot, the *Textus Roffensis*, *Hamlet*, Robinson's *Honest to God*, *The Canterbury Tales*, Holinshed's *Chronicle*, the Cathedral Statutes of Rochester, *Hymns Ancient and Modern* (Revised), Bonhoeffer's *Letters and Papers from Prison*, Hammersjkold's *Markings*, *The Thoughts of Chairman Mao*, *Pilgrim's Progress*, the *Sixteen Satires* of Juvenal and the *Book of Kells*" deprived of indications of date and authorship, all printed in the same format and bound together as a single volume.[1]

This diverse literary menu combined with the standardized print format can mislead interpreters. As Christian interpreters, they are convinced that every part of Scripture is equally "God-breathed" and therefore "useful for teaching, rebuking, correcting and training in righteousness" (2 Tim. 3:16). Accordingly, it is their sincere desire to make all of Scripture useful—that is, spiritually nourishing.

But to continue the food metaphor, we do not approach all food and beverage items in the same way. Some we drink, some we eat with a spoon and others with a fork, and for some we also need a sharp knife in order to be properly nourished by them. Similarly, we should not approach all literary genres in the same way, as if all of Scripture simply consisted of direct theological declarations from God—or inspired "mottos." Divine truth is communicated differently through a lament psalm than through a narrative in Judges, a group of commands in Deuteronomy, or a letter to the Asia Minor churches in Revelation 1–3. This means that we must approach each genre differently in order to derive spiritual nourishment from it. Failing to give sufficient attention to genre distinctions can lead to interpretive indigestion, that is, to misinterpreting and misapplying biblical texts. Theologian Kevin Vanhoozer explains the importance of understanding genre using a different metaphor:

> The Bible is composed of different kinds of literature, each of which maps the theodrama [the theological drama] in a distinctive way. Yet all maps are reliable: they correspond—in different ways!—to this or that aspect of what really is the case. They are not only compatible but complement one another. Maps are no good, however, unless you are oriented.[2]

Poetry

Distinguishing Features of Biblical Poetry

Approximately one-third of the Old Testament and a number of New Testament texts are written in the form of poetry. Just like classical and modern poetry, biblical poetry abounds in figurative expressions, though these can be found in prose as well. Unlike classical poetry, it lacks clear patterns of meter or rhyme. And, unlike modern free verse but similar to other well-known Middle Eastern texts, such as the Qur'an or the *Gilgamesh Epic*, biblical poetry displays a striking "parallelistic" structure. This involves the pairing of two or more lines, which are closely related to one another but not always synonymous.

These characteristics of biblical poetry can be illustrated by Psalm 1:

1 Blessed is the one who does not walk in step with the wicked
2 or stand in the way that sinners take
3 or sit in the company of mockers,
4 but whose delight is in the law of the LORD
5 and who meditates on his law day and night.
6 That person is like a tree planted by streams of water,
7 which yields its fruit in season
8 and whose leaf does not wither
9 —whatever they do prospers.
10 Not so the wicked!
11 They are like chaff that the wind blows away.
12 Therefore the wicked will not stand in the judgment,
13 nor sinners in the assembly of the righteous.
14 For the LORD watches over the way of the righteous,
15 but the way of the wicked leads to destruction.

The psalm begins and ends with a common biblical metaphor. Lines 1–3 and 14–15 develop the image of life as a journey. Lines 6–8 and 10–11 present two contrasting similes. The righteous (as they are identified in lines 13–14) are compared with a fruitful tree, and the wicked are compared with chaff. Line 9 clarifies lines 7–8 using plain language—like this tree, they are prospering, accomplishing what they were created to do.

The initial parallel lines (1–3) present a series of progressions. For example, the potential companion progresses from the "wicked," who simply disregard God's authority and commands, to "mockers," who actively oppose God and his followers. Lines 4–5 describe a positive attitude toward God's word in complementary terms. Lines 7–8 describe two signs of the tree's flourishing. Finally, lines 12–13 describe the final outcome for the wicked, while lines 14–15 account for the contrasting circumstances of the righteous and the wicked.

As our brief analysis of Psalm 1 illustrates, the pairing of parallel lines and figurative expressions, especially simile and metaphor, are prominent stylistic features of biblical poetry. Figurative language can enrich our understanding of a topic by providing vivid and concrete illustrations of what the text is trying to communicate. As we noted briefly in the preceding chapter, though, figurative statements can also be a source of misinterpretation if we fail to properly distinguish between what is *figurative* and what is *literal*. The metaphor of the path/journey in lines 1–3 warns us against following the ways of the wicked; it doesn't mean that we shouldn't spend any time around people who don't know God. And the simile of the tree in lines 6–9 helps to restrict the use of the word "prosper." The person who continually meditates on God's Word will be fruitful like a healthy tree—not fabulously wealthy!

Figurative Language

J. Matthew Sleeth takes the shepherd/sheep imagery in Psalm 23 literally when he tells us that this psalm informed us three thousand years ago that "the Lord restores our soul by leading us to streams and pastures." Since living "in a man-made world" is "making us ill," Sleeth responds: "What remedy does God prescribe for our souls? Still waters and green pastures."[3] Now it certainly can be refreshing to leave the noise and bustle of the city and spend some time in the countryside or out in nature, but Psalm 23 does not supply Sleeth with an ancient biblical warrant for this claim. The metaphor in the psalm describes sheep (which spend little time in busy urban streets)—not people—as needing to be led to restful pools and grassy pastures. After being guided through the sweltering wilderness, the sheep revive by being amply supplied with food and drink. This favorite biblical metaphor provides no support for Sleeth's environmental cause. The focus of the metaphor is on God, the wise and caring shepherd, who supplies us with all that we need rather than instructing us, the sheep, about how to care for ourselves.

Joshua Harris makes the opposite mistake in discussing Proverbs 7, taking figuratively what probably should be taken literally: "In Proverbs, foolishness is portrayed as a wicked seductress who lures her victim with the offer of romantic and sexual pleasures devoid of responsibility. 'Come, let's drink deep of love till morning,' she says, 'let's enjoy ourselves with love!' (Proverbs 7:18 [TNIV]). This is how foolishness works."[4] Now, it is true that wisdom is often portrayed in Proverbs 1–9 as a woman (1:20–33; 3:13–18; 4:5–9; 7:4–5; 8:1–36), and Lady Folly is contrasted with Lady Wisdom in chapter 9. In Proverbs 2:16–19; 5:3–6, 8–17; 6:24–35; 7:5–27, however, the adulteress or promiscuous woman is to be understood literally as a genuine temptation and threat to the young male who is being addressed (note the repeated references to "my son" in 2:1; 5:1; 6:20; 7:1). This woman is not a figurative portrayal of folly, just as the perverse men in Proverbs 2:12–15 and the loan seeker in 6:1–5 are to be understood not as personifications or symbols but as real people.

The Challenge of Prophetic Language

In the example above from Proverbs 7, it does not make much of a difference whether you take the description of the seductress literally or figuratively since Harris's point remains the same. In fact, taking the portrait literally would actually strengthen the point he is making about sexual intimacy during romance and courtship. In other examples, however, a literal/figurative confusion can lead an interpreter to take what is addressed to a nation and appropriate it personally. This occurs when John Eldredge quotes Jeremiah 31:21: "Set up road signs; put up guideposts. Take note of the highway, the road that you take." The reference to "road signs" should probably be understood fairly literally as encouraging the exiled Israelites to prepare to return not only to their God but also to their beloved homeland. This is suggested by the second half of the verse ("Return, Virgin Israel, return to your towns"), and verse 17 clearly indicates: "'So there is hope for your descendants,' declares the LORD. 'Your children will return to their own land.'" Eldredge, however, takes the first half of Jeremiah 31:21 figuratively as a personal word of guidance from God instructing him to write a book "on the stages of the masculine journey."[5]

As this example illustrates, the often personal and emotional tone of prophetic rhetoric can encourage individuals to apply these texts to themselves. Popular treatments of the Old Testament prophets often focus on their predictions of the first and second comings of Jesus as Messiah and on the signs pointing to the end of time as we know it, as popularized by the Left Behind series of prophetic fiction novels. Many prophetic texts, however, emphasize God's nature, his covenantal promises to his people, and his expectations and demands of them. To the extent that the Christian church is in continuity with and thus the heir to these promises, it is fitting that believers today make ample use of them. The New Testament writers did the same. Note how Peter uses Isaiah 40:6–8 in 1 Peter 1:24–25: "For, 'All people are like grass, and all their glory is like the flowers of the field; the grass withers and the flowers fall, but the word of the Lord endures forever.' And this is the word that was preached to you." Paul uses the same chapter in an equally direct manner: "The person with the Spirit makes judgments about all things, but such a person is not subject to merely human judgments, for, 'Who has known the mind of the Lord so as to instruct him?' But we have the mind of Christ" (1 Cor. 2:15–16, citing Isa. 40:13; see also Rom. 11:33–34). And he quotes Isaiah 59:7–8 in Romans 3, along with other Old Testament texts, to describe sinful humanity: "Their feet are swift to shed blood; ruin and misery mark their ways, and the way of peace they do not know" (vv. 15–17).

Claiming Someone Else's Promises

When using prophetic books, however, it is necessary to determine as far as possible who *specifically* is being addressed by a given text and in what situation. Then we may evaluate how these factors, in turn, shape and restrict the way we may appropriately use the text in our lives today. Rick Warren in his *Purpose Driven Life* simply assumes that Isaiah 44:2a ("I am your Creator. You were in my care even before you were born" [CEV]) and 46:3b–4 can be taken as addressing any human being rather than being limited to Israel in exile.[6] In these texts the prophet is using the metaphor of human birth to portray God's long-term loving involvement in Israel's history as a people and nation. This is clearly indicated by the surrounding verses, which Warren conveniently leaves out: "People of Israel, I have chosen you as my servant. . . . Israel, don't be terrified! You are my chosen servant, my very favorite" (Isa. 44:1–2 CEV) and "You survivors in Israel, listen to me, the LORD" (Isa. 46:3 CEV).

Psalm 139, which Warren also cites here, indicates that the claims of these texts in Isaiah are generally true of individuals as well. Therefore, Warren is not using these texts to support something that is not found elsewhere in Scripture. He does, however, use Isaiah 46:3–4 (NCV) to demonstrate that God "wanted to make you in order to express his love," which these verses do not state or even imply.[7]

Another prophetic promise that is commonly claimed today as a general promise for all believers is Jeremiah 29:11. Bill Sanders cites it in a book written to encourage the parents of teens:

> If we would only trust God and his words in this passage, we would have such joy that all the words in the dictionary could not fully describe it. Give your cares to the Lord and bathe in the beauty of his love.
>
> "For I know the plans I have for you," says the Lord. "They are plans for good and not for disaster, to give you a future and a hope." (Jeremiah 29:11 [NLT])
>
> Your loving Father wants to cuddle you in his love. All of his plans for you are good. Don't let the lies of this age or your past keep you prisoner for even another second.[8]

I vividly recall a time in the life of our family when we were in the midst of an uncertain transition. A children's music tape brought this verse to my attention for the first time, and my wife and I ended up singing the Jeremiah 29:11 song again and again while doing the dishes. It never occurred to me to look up the verse and see who initially received this promise. A children's chorus from the 1950s boasts, "Every promise in the Book is mine; Every chapter, every verse, every line; All are blessings of His love divine, Every promise in the Book is mine." But this is not true if a specific biblical promise is limited to a particular addressee or time or if it depends on a condition that I am unwilling or unable to fulfill.

Not all Christian writers agree with this conclusion. Jack E. Shaw responds quite differently to this song: "My faith in God's promises began early in my life. One of my favorite Sunday School songs expresses it like this: . . . Claim God's promises to you. Believe—and receive: 'No good thing does he withhold from those whose walk is blameless' (Ps. 84:11 NIV)."⁹ But consider this promise given to the prophet Hosea: "Yet I will show love to Judah; and I will save them—not by bow, sword or battle, or by horses and horsemen, but I, the LORD their God, will save them" (Hosea 1:7). This promise was directed to the southern kingdom of Judah (just as Hosea 1:6 is directed to the northern kingdom of Israel), probably in conjunction with the Assyrian siege of 701 BC, as described in 2 Kings 19. Hosea 1:7 is clearly not *my* promise. An even clearer example is found in 2 Kings 20:5–6 (CEV): "The LORD sent him back to Hezekiah with this message: Hezekiah, . . . I heard you pray, and I saw you cry. I will heal you, so that three days from now you will be able to worship in my temple. I will let you live fifteen years more, while I protect you and your city from the king of Assyria." In this case, probably few would dispute that this promise was made to Hezekiah and no one else. On what basis then should we view Hosea 1:7 any differently?

What about Jeremiah 29:11 then? The first verse of the chapter identifies the original recipients of this promise: "This is the text of the letter that the prophet Jeremiah sent from Jerusalem to the surviving elders among the exiles and to the priests, the prophets and all the other people Nebuchadnezzar had carried into exile from Jerusalem to Babylon." During the seven decades of the exile, they were to settle down and make themselves at home in Mesopotamia, building houses, planting gardens, marrying and raising children, and even praying for the well-being of the conquering enemy's capital city, while ignoring the false prophets' empty promises (vv. 5–9). Directly preceding the much-cited verse 11, God gives the exiles a specific promise in verse 10: "This is what the LORD says: 'When seventy years are completed for Babylon, I will come to you and fulfill my good promise to bring you back to this place'" (Jerusalem, where the letter was composed). This promise of a return to Jerusalem is what verse 11 then describes as God's ultimate "plans to prosper you and not to harm you," speaking directly to the exiles from Judah.

The also much-cited affirmations of Romans 8:28–32 confirm that the promise directed to the Judean exiles in Jeremiah 29:11 reflects the way that God generally deals with his people, as in the case of Isaiah 44:2a and 46:3b–4 discussed above. So to apply the promise of Jeremiah 29:11 to encourage others in their present difficult situations is not contrary to the spirit of this text even if they are not the original recipients. Nevertheless, keeping the original context of the promise in mind can help to guard us against misusing the text, for instance, by understanding the word "prosper" (NIV) in terms of the "health and wealth gospel." The Hebrew word used here, *shalom* ("well-being"), is much broader and always expresses a divine gift rather than a human achievement. Attending to the context also reminds us that, even though those exiled from Judah to Babylon may not have experienced any further harm there, many of their former fellow citizens in Jerusalem did not fare as well when the Babylonian army conquered that city. Reading the book of Lamentations and remembering the thousands of modern-day Christian martyrs offers a helpful corrective against simplistically claiming the promise of protection from harm! We will discuss the proper application of biblical texts more fully in the next chapter.

Historical Narrative

One of the most appealing biblical genres is historical narrative. It is found in more than half of the Old Testament books, as well as in the four Gospels and Acts in the New Testament. Biblical narratives are artistic literary compositions that are more like short stories than archival reports. They present the challenges of the life of faith in a multifaceted portrait, which often mirrors our own struggles and triumphs. This can lead to a number of problems in interpretation and application. We already discussed in chapter 3 the tendency to read a specific narrative in isolation from its larger context. There is also a temptation to derive a moral from each individual story, much like an Aesop fable, or to suppose that even minor details have spiritual importance. Another major problem arises when we assume that what is *described* in the narrative is *prescribed* by God by virtue of being a part of inspired Scripture. Or, in other words, we may wrongly believe that we should aspire to do whatever the biblical characters did. The examples below illustrate these issues.

Confusing the Descriptive for the Prescriptive

Gary Smalley and John Trent's book *The Blessing* encourages parents to make it a priority to bless their children, based on the model of the patriarchal blessing in Genesis 27 and 48–49. The authors correctly acknowledge that the patriarchal blessing played a unique role in salvation history. It was reserved for one special occasion, it was irrevocable and prophetic, and it was based on God's sovereign choice of the biological line of divine blessing. Smalley and Trent are convinced, however, that these passages not only portray the actions of Isaac and Jacob but also teach the permanent importance of parental blessing. They even identify in Genesis five elements that every parental blessing should include: giving a meaningful touch, delivering a spoken message, attaching high value to the person being blessed, picturing a special future for that person, and being actively committed to helping to fulfill that blessing.[10]

Smalley and Trent's approach reflects a basic misunderstanding of how biblical narratives communicate spiritual truth. To move properly from what the narrative describes the biblical characters doing to what is prescribed for us to do, it is important, first of all, to identify the narrative's place within the larger biblical story of redemption. As we do that, we should keep the focus on God and his involvement in history, not on the deeds of biblical heroes and heroines (or villains). We should be cautious about deriving theology or practices directly from narrative description because the narrative does not always make it clear which of the biblical characters' beliefs and practices we should follow. Should we also follow the patriarchs in practicing polygamy (Gen. 16:1–4; 29:15–30) and lying to get ourselves out of tight spots (Gen. 12:10–20; 20:1–18; 26:1–11)? Since narratives "illustrate what is taught explicitly and categorically elsewhere,"[11] we are better off basing our theology and practices on the explicit teachings of Scripture. When reading narratives, we should pay attention to how the details were selected and ordered. This will help us see how they portray the nature of genuine faith and obedience in the interplay between divine sovereignty and human responsibility.

The dominant theme of the book of Genesis is God's sovereign election, preparation, and preservation of a covenant family as a part of his plan to counteract the devastating effects of sin. This covenant family will serve as a channel of divine blessing to all the nations. When a patriarch blessed a son, he was simply acknowledging what God had already determined and promised to do. Unfortunately, the patriarch could be tricked, or he could be swayed by his own prejudices. The fact that only one son per family (and never a daughter) was singled out to receive the primary blessing suggests that these texts do not offer a paradigm for Christian parenting. Nor can a patriarch who offers a blessing on his deathbed be viewed as someone who was actively committed to seeing the blessing fulfilled.

There is no indication that Abraham officially blessed his son Isaac, and outside of the book of Genesis, there is not a single blessing by a father over a son recorded anywhere else in the Old Testament. This suggests that the patriarchal blessing was a unique, pre-Sinai, patriarchal ceremony rather than a model for us today. The closest parallel to the patriarchal blessing outside of Genesis is Moses's blessing of the tribes of Israel (Deut. 33). This may indicate that God's means of passing on the divine blessing had already changed by Moses's day. The fact that Smalley and Trent turn to Psalms and Proverbs for sample blessings suggests that the prayers, words of encouragement, and optimistic wishes of contemporary Christian fathers (and mothers) have little in common with the patriarchal blessing. As Christian parents, seeking to contribute to the spiritual development of our children in any way possible is certainly biblical—but not because it is commanded or commended in the book of Genesis.

Eugene Peterson offers another example of this approach in claiming that the call of Samuel in 1 Samuel 3 serves as "a paradigm for the adolescent experience" by grounding it "in a theological setting." In Peterson's opinion, this text has clear implications for how parents should deal with their teenage children: "the parent is not in charge of the so-called identity crisis." Instead, God is in charge since Samuel's call occurred when he was alone at night, and Eli is commended for being "quite willing to trust Samuel to that solitude." This text thus "provides a window through which the Christian can see that the most significant reality in adolescent development is a relationship with God." Samuel moved from childhood to adulthood when he "acknowledged that *God* was calling his name" and recognized himself not as "a child of Elkanah and Hannah, not the ward of Eli, but the one God calls by personal name."[12]

Peterson's approach is clearly anachronistic. He reads modern psychological views of adolescence and identity crisis into an ancient text whose author was probably unaware of these categories and concerns. In his effort to develop a biblical approach to parenting teenagers, Peterson ignores how this text functions within the larger biblical narrative. Samuel is an extraordinary prophet, priest, and statesman whom God uniquely calls at a young age to help usher in a new era in redemptive history—the monarchy. For Peterson, however, he becomes a representative adolescent, an "everyman" figure. Moreover, if Eli's treatment of Samuel is made normative, how should we deal with his parenting of his own evil sons (1 Sam. 2:29; 3:12–13)? Should all parents send their children off to a religious "boarding school" at a young age because that's what Samuel's parents did (1 Sam. 1:24–28), with the apparent approval of the biblical author? Rather than reading modern principles of adolescent identity formation into 1 Samuel 3, we should note how the author contrasts Samuel and his parents with Eli and his sons (2:12–36 and 3:11–14). Hearing God's call did not suddenly move Samuel from childhood to adulthood; following this encounter he still had to "grow up" (1 Sam. 3:19). This text emphasizes God's judgment on blatant sin in the family of Eli, Israel's religious leader. It also portrays God's careful preparation of Samuel for significant spiritual and political leadership as one who was open to hearing God's voice and obeying.

The effort to find a biblical basis for contemporary secular theories and church practices can sometimes lead interpreters to ascribe great significance to minor textual details. Several years ago, I heard a speaker on a Christian family radio broadcast discussing Judges 13, in which an "angel of the LORD" imposes a Nazirite vow on Manoah's previously infertile wife, requiring her to abstain from alcohol for the duration of her abruptly announced pregnancy. The speaker claimed that the reason for the angel's instruction was that he knew of the physical damage that alcohol can do. In other words, the purpose of the Nazirite vow was to prevent Samson from suffering from "fetal alcohol syndrome." The speaker did not explain, however, why no other Hebrew mother received a similar warning or why Samson was called to live by the Nazirite vow for his entire life.

Spiritualizing Narrative Details

The desire to derive a spiritually edifying message from narrative texts can also lead interpreters to spiritualize them, a not-too-distant cousin of the allegorizing approach of the early church. For example, Joshua's conquest of Jericho (Josh. 6) becomes a picture of spiritual victory in our everyday life, as the walls that are holding us back tumble down. Or the jars of oil in 2 Kings 4:1–7 become areas of our life filled by the Holy Spirit.

I vividly recall my first sermon in my home church midweek prayer meeting when I preached a "missionary" message from 2 Kings 7. In this passage, a group of lepers discovers the sudden departure of the

Aramean army that has been besieging Samaria and begins to enjoy the plunder the army left behind. "Then they said to each other, 'What we're doing is not right. *This is a day of good news and we are keeping it to ourselves.* If we wait until daylight, punishment will overtake us. Let's go at once and report this to the royal palace'" (v. 9, italics added). In my sermon I transformed the lepers who announced Samaria's military victory into evangelists. (I would handle the text differently today!)

What's wrong with this approach? First, it implies that the narratives themselves present no theological message about God's purposes for humanity in general and his elect people in particular or about how we should respond. Second Timothy 3:16–17, in affirming that Old Testament texts, including narratives, are useful for doctrinal and ethical instruction, gives no indication that these texts first need to be "spiritualized." Second, as a result, a "spiritualizing" interpreter usually sees no need to carefully analyze the context and understand its details in light of their original historical-cultural setting. What the text *meant* to its original readers becomes largely irrelevant as long as it *means* something to us today. Third, little effort is made to reflect how the text illustrates *by means of story*[13] what is taught by means of direct instruction elsewhere in the Bible. Finally, as the preceding examples illustrate, like allegory, there is often no objective control on how an interpreter determines the correct spiritual equivalents of the mundane details of the text.

Rather than carefully interpreting the biblical narrative, this approach typically involves suggesting contemporary spiritual equivalents for the central events in a given narrative. John Maxwell, for example, in a book on Christian leadership development, quotes the story of David and Goliath from 1 Samuel 17. He emphasizes verse 52a—"Then the men of Israel and Judah surged forward with a shout and pursued the Philistines"—which he considers to be "the key to the whole story. The reason we need to kill the giants in our lives is this: those whom we lead will never kill the giants in their lives until we first kill the giants in our lives."[14] But even a superficial examination of the surrounding context indicates that 1 Samuel 17 serves to validate Samuel in anointing David to be Israel's next king (16:12–13) and Saul in selecting David as his courtier-musician (16:17–19). David's actions also serve to contrast him with terror-filled Saul whose armor he refuses to wear (17:11, 38–39) and who was selected as king specifically to lead the Israelites into battle against their enemies

(8:20). It appears that Maxwell designates verse 52a as the key to the story because it serves as the basis for the contemporary application he wishes to make.

Maxwell also labels his five strategies for "giant killing" as "five stones." He leaves it up to his readers to identify their own personal giant, which he more appropriately labels elsewhere as a "seemingly insurmountable barrier."[15] In the process, however, he ignores the fact that after David killed Goliath, there apparently were no other giants left on the immediate battlefield for the Israelites to kill,[16] and the Philistine troops began to flee even before the Israelites arose to give chase. David killed Goliath so that the Israelites didn't have to face the giant themselves. Furthermore, Goliath wasn't any Israelite citizen's *personal* threat—especially not David's—but was merely the champion of the Philistine army, which threatened Israel as a whole. If we label our personal difficulties "our giant" (be it a difficult math class, a strained marriage, an unreasonable boss, or a Sunday school class of unruly middle school boys), we run the risk of overly dramatizing both our problems and what is involved in "killing" any of these foes.

Maxwell's use of 1 Samuel 17 also illustrates how interpreters tend to turn the biblical characters into spiritual heroes to emulate (or spiritual failures whose mistakes we should avoid), rather than focusing on God and his involvement in history. It is clear that David's actions in confronting Goliath are contrasted with King Saul's fear and resultant inaction (v. 11). But David's speech before Saul prior to the one-on-one battle does not highlight his courage and military heroism. Instead, it expresses David's desire to defend God's reputation (v. 36, compare v. 26) and his utter confidence that the God who delivered him from past danger would deliver him in the ensuing battle (v. 37). His words to Goliath state the same convictions even more emphatically (vv. 45–47), leaving no doubt that David is relying completely on God to grant him victory, not on his own skills, despite the fact that in such combat, David's skill with the sling gives him a strategic advantage since he can strike Goliath before Goliath can strike him.

Some recent theoretical discussions of how to apply biblical narratives emphasize deriving timeless, universal principles from these texts. Others encourage the believer to study multiple texts in order to understand what God is like, what his purposes in the world are, who we are as God's people, and how we should act today in the ongoing drama of redemption.[17] Whether we follow the former or the latter model, a text like 1 Samuel 17 encourages us to trust God, even in situations that look hopeless, but it offers no guarantee that he will always deliver us (see, for example, Dan. 3:17–18). In the end, this may not sound radically different from spiritualizing approaches, but it avoids the fanciful and unrestrained effort to identify contemporary "giants," "slings," "stones," and "unfamiliar armor."

Finding Christ Everywhere in the Old Testament

A somewhat more radical approach to interpreting Old Testament narratives involves reading them as foreshadowing the life and ministry of Christ and his church. Viewing the Bible as "an extraordinary love letter," S. J. Hill sees in the narratives of the Old Testament many a "prophetic portrait of Christ and his bride" or of "the Father's relationship with Jesus."[18] Christian interpreters throughout history have noted a parallel between Abraham's near sacrifice of Isaac and God the Father's offering of his Son Jesus to be crucified, even though no New Testament author confirms the significance of this parallel. Hill, however, sees even more parallels in the narratives of Abraham and Isaac, focusing on the love affair between Isaac and Rebekah. According to Hill, "what appears on the surface to be nothing more than a curious tale about a father's desire to find a wife for a son is really a striking illustration of God's passion to pursue a people for the sake of His beloved Son." Accordingly, the servant's role in Genesis 24—for example, in taking gifts along with him (v. 10)—"is similar to the Holy Spirit's role in the earth." And just as Rebekah was willing to follow the servant back to marry Isaac sight unseen, we should "become eager to follow the Holy Spirit on a journey through the wilderness of this fallen world to a place we've never been in order to be wed to Someone we've never seen."[19]

What should we make of such an interpretation? It is apparent that Hill finds no spiritual point in the Genesis narrative apart from his Christ-focused analogy. He is so caught up in preaching Christ from the Old Testament that he has completely lost sight of the Old Testament as God's inspired, authoritative Word apart from any such analogy. It is true that the New Testament, especially the book of Hebrews, sees numerous connections between the two testaments based on typology. Typology is the idea that God used particular Old Testament events, people, roles, and rituals both to accomplish his purposes for Israel and as models (or "types") to foreshadow a greater reality that was to come in the future with Jesus Christ.[20] Hebrews focuses especially on how Israel's sacrificial system as administered by the priests pointed forward to the atoning work of Jesus. There is an ongoing debate about whether—or to what extent—we should scour the Old Testament for additional "types" that are not noted in the New Testament. Hill, however, fails to acknowledge how God accomplished his purposes for Israel's ancestors through their lives and marriages, as recounted, for example, in Genesis 24.

The alternative is not to turn this text into a paradigm of how to find a godly wife, as one speaker did in a Wheaton College chapel some years ago. Isaac and Rebekah hardly enjoyed a model marriage. Just consider how she later deceived her husband in order to obtain his blessing for her favorite son, Jacob! She was even willing to be cursed by God in order to get her way and block her husband's intention to give the blessing to Esau (Gen. 27:13). When we read these narratives, we should focus instead on the larger context of God's covenantal promise to Abraham and Sarah that he would bless the nations through their offspring (Gen. 22:17–18). This, in turn, required that they have children. Accordingly, many of the chapters of Genesis serve to relate how God enlarged and preserved the extended family of Abraham and Sarah, despite infertility, potentially dangerous foreign sojourns, and human intrigue and doubt.

Genesis 24 is a remarkably detailed chapter (with sixty-seven verses—the thirteenth longest in the Bible by verse count) describing how a wife was chosen for Isaac when Abraham was very old (v. 1). This made it possible for the covenantal promise to continue beyond Isaac. The text emphasizes God's guidance in the affair—Abraham relies on it (v. 7, 40) and the servant prays for it (vv. 12–15, 42–44) and subsequently gives thanks for having received it (vv. 26–27, 48). Here we also need to note that the servant is not asking God to direct him to the godliest potential wife for Isaac out of all of the women then alive but rather to help him select one from among Abraham's close relatives (vv. 4, 40). In other words, "Abraham made this requirement for ethnic reasons, not for spiritual reasons. His family had been polytheistic. No one else in the world in this time worshiped Abraham's God."[21] This text, therefore, does not teach us anything about the bride of Christ. Nor does it give us guidance about how to seek a godly bride today, for example, by giving God specific instructions on how to point her out to us (vv. 14, 43–44). Instead, it illustrates how God faithfully keeps his promises to his people and answers prayer.

Avoiding Common Fallacies in Applying Narrative Texts

John and Kim Walton have noted five common fallacies in attempts to derive life lessons from biblical narratives (and other genres) for Sunday school curriculum. Such lessons lack true scriptural authority because they fail to respect the intentions of the biblical authors:[22]

1. **Promotion of the trivial** (basing the lesson on a passing comment)
2. **Illegitimate extrapolation** (expanding the lesson from a specific situation to all situations)
3. **Reading between the lines** (deriving the lesson from the reader's speculations about the characters' unexpressed thoughts and motivations)
4. **Missing important nuance** (pinpointing an appropriate but incomplete lesson, since it neglects a crucial theological connection)
5. **Focus on people rather than on God** (emphasizing the characters' actions in identifying the lesson rather than God's involvement in the events)

As we have noted above, all of these fallacies are prominent in the use of the Bible in popular Christian books. I have treated narrative more fully than other biblical genres because interpreters draw on it so frequently—and often in questionable ways. In the process, I have commended an alternative approach to transforming narrative description into ethical prescription, as well as to the strategies of allegorizing and moralizing.

Our primary goal when interpreting a biblical narrative is to determine the emphasis of the text by paying close attention to details such as plot and character development, dialogue and explanations, the arrangement of scenes, repetition of key terms, and allusions to other biblical texts, in addition to its literary context. Only then are we prepared to derive a spiritual lesson from that emphasis. We should take care that we do not too readily equate our world and our faith struggles with those portrayed in the Bible. Instead, we should note how these stories give us a framework for viewing our lives as also part of God's redemptive plan by illustrating the nature of the life of faith and obedience in ways that are comparable to our own challenges and experiences.

Let me briefly illustrate this process from 1 Samuel 25, the fascinating account of how Abigail saves her family from being slain by an angry David and ends up becoming his wife. The immediate context already points us toward the author's point. This chapter is placed between two narratives (1 Sam. 24 and 26) in which David spares Saul's life because he is God's chosen king (24:7, 10; 26:9, 11, 23), despite the fact that Saul is seeking to kill him. Yet in the case of Nabal, a wealthy owner of sheep and goats, David is prepared to wipe him out without hesitation for rebuffing and insulting him. The chapter begins by describing in verse 3 the contrasting characters of Abigail ("intelligent and beautiful") and Nabal ("surly and mean"), alerting us to the kind of behavior we may expect from them. David is also contrasted with both Saul and Nabal. The plot revolves around the question of whether David will succeed in killing Nabal and his family, thus repaying evil with evil, or be stopped by Abigail. The central contrast here is between good and evil actions (25:3, 15, 17, 21, 26, 28, 30–31, 34, 39). Abigail, however, succeeds in convincing David that taking revenge is wrong and conflicts with God's purposes for his life (25:26, 31, 33, 39).

God's direct role in dealing with Nabal (vv. 37–38) and in using Abigail to restrain David from killing innocent people (vv. 26, 33) is emphasized in David's words of praise upon hearing of Nabal's sudden demise (v. 39). These points are also reinforced by allusions to the larger David narrative (compare v. 28 with 1 Sam. 18:17 and 2 Sam. 7:16; v. 29 with 1 Sam. 17:40, 49–50; and v. 30 with 1 Sam. 13:14). This narrative illustrates the folly of seeking personal revenge rather than committing our situation to God when mistreated, as set forth in Romans 12:17–21. It also demonstrates how wise individuals can help to restrain evil. These lessons have broad applications without turning the six menu items bountifully supplied by Abigail (v. 18) into six categories of timely deeds!

Old Testament Laws

Although we have given special attention to narratives, each biblical genre presents its own interpretive challenges and its own possibilities for proper and improper application. In interpreting Old Testament legal texts, we may sometimes be unaware of social or cultural background information that is helpful to know in order to understand how a specific law functioned in ancient Israel. This can lead us to read these texts in light of contemporary cultural values. In many cases, unfortunately, the Bible itself offers little explanation of the rationale for a given law. And often we can't be certain whether suggested background considerations are correct. Furthermore, we can forget that Israelite laws were embedded in Israel's covenantal relationship with God and thus have little in common with our local laws and regulations.

We should note here that the books of Exodus, Leviticus, Numbers, and Deuteronomy do not consist exclusively of law collections. They also contain numerous narratives describing Israel's deliverance from the Egyptians and subsequent rebellions and wanderings in the wilderness, as well as exhortations to serve God with joy and obey the law. In a book promoting "good eating," Stephen Webb mistakenly derives ethical guidelines from one of these exhortations when he identifies in Deuteronomy 8:7–10 "the ideal diet for the Hebrews"—a vegetarian diet that excludes meat. These verses state: "For the LORD your God is bringing you into a good land—a land with brooks, streams, and deep springs gushing out into the valleys and hills; a land with wheat and barley, vines and fig trees, pomegranates, olive oil and honey; a land where bread will not be scarce and you will lack nothing; a land where the rocks are iron and you can dig copper out of the hills. When you have eaten and are satisfied, praise the LORD your God for the good land he has given you."[23]

The mention of iron and copper here makes it clear that this text is not *prescribing* an ideal diet but merely *describing* the abundant natural resources of the Promised Land that the Israelites are about to enter. Such a list would not include domesticated animals. More to the point, numerous legal texts describing sacrifices other than the burnt offering (for example, Lev. 1:3) clearly permit a sacrificial or otherwise slaughtered animal to be eaten. Depending on the type of sacrifice or situation, part of the animal can be eaten by the priest, the one bringing the sacrifice, a group of friends, or the needy (Lev. 6:16, 26; 7:19; 11:2–3, 9, 21–22; 22:13; Deut. 12:15, 20–22; 14:23, 26, 29; 15:19–22; 16:6–7).

On a related issue, Michael Jacobson is convinced that the divine command against eating fat as stated in Leviticus 3:16–17 and 7:23 is due to health concerns. In his view, "God's commandment prohibiting the eating of animal fat was His loving protection for His people and was at least one major reason for his declaring that those who ate it would be 'cut off.'" God as "the original Ph.D. of Biochemistry" knew the danger of foods that are high in long-chain saturated fat and therefore forbade them—and so should we.[24] Jacobson acknowledges that the fat of venison was not forbidden but assumes that this was because deer were undomesticated and therefore lean. We already discussed this prohibition in the previous chapter. Here it is sufficient to note that Jacobson could be correct, but there is no clear scriptural evidence to support his conclusion. And it is likely that other factors were also involved.[25] The term "cut off" (Lev. 7:20–21) likely refers to divine judgment, leading to the immediate death of the sinning individual.[26] If so, there is some irony in protecting people's health by threatening them with divine execution if they eat any meat containing harmful long-chain fats!

Some Christian interpreters simply dismiss the Old Testament law as having been done away with in Jesus, citing verses like Romans 10:4: "For Christ is the end of the law for righteousness to everyone who believes" (ESV, HCSB, NKJV). Most, however, seek to determine the implications of the Mosaic law for contemporary Christian ethics. After all, didn't Jesus warn that "anyone who sets aside one of the least of these commands and teaches others accordingly will be called least in the kingdom of heaven" (Matt. 5:19)? Also, Jesus and the various New Testament authors make extensive use of Old Testament laws in grounding their moral instructions. (See, for example, the use of Exod. 20:13–14; 21:24; Lev. 19:18; and Deut. 24:1 in Matt. 5:21–48 and Paul's use of Deut. 5:16 in Eph. 6:1–3.)

One well-known disputed law is Leviticus 19:28: "Do not cut your bodies for the dead or put tattoo marks on yourselves. I am the LORD." On the one side, there are those who view this as a universal, timeless prohibition. Eloise Choice categorically states: "God does not want mankind to wear tattoos. Satan and his legions utilized cuttings in the flesh and marks on the flesh of man as well as specified hair and beard-cuts and designs, to determine which humans belonged to which devils."[27] Betty Miller agrees: "The Bible warns against tattoos in Leviticus 19:28. . . . Other scriptures, such as 1 Kings 18:28 and Deuteronomy 14:1, also warn us not to disfigure our bodies. . . . Tattooing has its origin in witchcraft practices. That's what makes it spiritually dangerous."[28]

On the other side, there are those who wear and advocate "Christian" tattoos—in fact, there is even a Christian Tattoo Association. In defense of their position, they point out that some of the verses surrounding this prohibition in Leviticus 19 contain commands that almost no Christian considers binding on us today. For example, the verse that immediately precedes states: "Do not cut the hair at the sides of your head or clip off the edges of your beard" (v. 27). This is too simple an argument, however, for the following verse states: "Do not degrade your daughter by making her a prostitute, or the land will turn to prostitution and be filled with wickedness" (v. 29). Certainly many Christians would see this verse as still relevant to us today! So how do we decide whether the prohibition against tattoos is like the command about haircutting rather than the one about prostitution? In other words, how do we determine which commands are still binding on us as Christians and how they apply to our lives?

In dealing with legal texts like this, we should begin by seeking any indications in the text about how the command might have functioned in ancient Israel. The tattoo prohibition in Leviticus 19:28, for example, is in the midst of a section that prohibits certain ways of cutting hair (v. 27), occult practices (vv. 26, 31), and (sacred) prostitution (v. 29), while commanding Sabbath observance and reverence for God's sanctuary (v. 30). This suggests that marking the body with tattoos was part of a pagan religious ritual in Old Testament times rather than simply a cosmetic procedure. Even though tattoos today may serve no comparable religious purpose, this does not resolve the question of whether we should avoid getting a tattoo today because of its claimed pagan origin. In any case, in dealing with obscure laws like Leviticus 19:28, it is probably wiser to offer a qualified opinion than a dogmatic conviction.

Proverbs

Another biblical genre that is often misused by popular interpreters is the wisdom proverb. Biblical proverbs should not be understood as divine *promises* that God has committed himself to fulfill but merely as spiritual *probabilities* that frequently result when a person follows the way of wisdom. We must remember that in a fallen world filled with fools and sinners, wise and godly behavior is not always crowned by acclaim, success, and prosperity. Nor is foolish and ungodly behavior always punished immediately. Henry Cloud and John Townsend seem to misunderstand the proverbial principle "a man reaps what he sows" (Gal. 6:7; compare Prov. 22:8) as a divine law. They argue that no one, including a parent, should counter this principle by preventing the expected consequences of a person's behavior from occurring.[29]

Fortunately, due to the interventions of divine grace, we often do *not* reap what we sow.

The proverb, which is the basic form of wisdom literature, has been defined as "a short, salty, concrete, fixed, paradigmatic, poetically-crafted saying."[30] This combination of features makes individual proverbs notoriously difficult to translate and interpret. Therefore, they are easily misused by interpreters who are unfamiliar with the underlying beliefs and characteristic vocabulary of wisdom sayings. In the words of Christian counselor and Old Testament scholar George Schwab, "Proverbs is too often treated as a proof-text source to sanction psychological theories" without adequate attention being paid to "the deep structure and central message of the book."[31]

This problem is illustrated vividly by Proverbs 22:6: "Start children off on the way they should go, and even when they are old they will not turn from it."[32] This verse is a favorite of Christian family counselors. The various ways in which Christian psychologists and counselors have interpreted this familiar proverb, as noted below, suggest that their counseling theories have influenced their understanding. How many parents have felt like failures because this promise did not prove true in their children's lives, leading them to conclude that they did not raise them properly?

This traditional understanding of Proverbs 22:6 nearly becomes Paul Meier's motto on parenting, especially regarding the first six years of life.[33] It is highly unlikely, however, that the Hebrew noun *na'ar* in this verse (sometimes translated "child") refers primarily to preschoolers as Meier suggests. It is more accurate to translate *na'ar* as "young man" in Proverbs because the person to whom the book is addressed is old enough to study these teachings (Prov. 1:4; the NIV translates the word here as "the young") and to be seduced by an adulteress (Prov. 7:7). Henry Cloud and John Townsend offer another interpretation: "The verse actually means 'the way God has planned for him (or her) to go,'" that is, the specific plan that "God intended for them."[34] Smalley and Trent suggest translating "according to his bent," meaning that we are to take a personal interest in each child we train (or bless), knowing the child's unique set of needs.[35] Neither of these suggestions is a probable option for understanding "way" in this context. It is unlikely that such a modern emphasis on a tailor-made upbringing that is sensitive to the divine calling or personal idiosyncrasies of each individual would have a place in ancient Israel's community-oriented ethic.

Robert Hicks focuses on the word translated here as "start off"—or more commonly "train up"—rather than on the word "way." Citing a similar Arabic word that means "to rub a child's palate with dates," he concludes that the Hebrew word used here (*chanak*) has to do with awakening one's appetite. He thus claims that the verse encourages parents to give children varied initiatory "experiences in the way of wisdom,"[36] hoping that they will embrace it for themselves. Unfortunately, this is a highly speculative and unproven etymology that gives us no clear guidance regarding how the word is used in biblical Hebrew.[37] Old Testament scholar Ted Hildebrandt points out that all of these interpretations overlook the more restrictive meanings of the three key terms in Proverbs 22:6 (that is, "initiate," "youth," "way"). After reviewing numerous possible interpretations and considering the proverb's historical-cultural background, Hildebrandt offers an interpretive paraphrase of the verse that could be expressed today as follows: If you are charged with raising Prince William of England, you need to give priority to preparing him for the unique role and responsibilities that will be his as long as he lives.[38]

The concise language of Proverbs sometimes lends itself to a wide range of suggested translations, resulting in some widely divergent applications. For example, the traditional translation of Proverbs 23:7—"as he thinks within himself/in his heart, so is he" (NASB, NKJV)—has inspired several entire books on the profound effect of our thought lives.[39] But it is unclear that this is the correct translation for this verse. According to the NIV, "he is the kind of person who is always thinking about the cost" (that is, of the meal he is hosting; the ESV and NLT are similar), while the NRSV translates it "for like a hair in the throat, so are they" (that is, they make you feel like vomiting)—a far cry from characterizing someone's inner thought life![40] In order to avoid the danger of building too much on a debatable translation, it is helpful to compare several published translations of a given proverb and to consult a commentary or two about interpretive options.

New Testament Epistles

Readers of Paul's letters often tend to assume that what he wrote to one first-century church as an inspired apostle applies to all modern churches as well. But New Testament scholar Gordon Fee emphasizes that these letters were written in response to particular occasions: "Usually the occasion was some kind of behavior that needed correcting, or a doctrinal error that needed setting right, or a misunderstanding that needed further light." As a result, the epistles offer "theology applied to or directed toward a particular need"—what Fee calls "task theology."[41] This means that what the apostle writes is not necessarily intended to address the long-term needs of the church universal, much less the personal concerns of individual believers today. These considerations complicate the interpretation of what otherwise appears to be the one biblical genre that we can apply directly to our lives.

One example of the failure to respect the occasional nature of New Testament letters is Robert Lewis's use of Hebrews 12:1–2 (Jesus enduring the pain and humiliation of crucifixion) and Hebrews 11:24–26 (Moses enduring "ill-treatment with the people of God") to derive the "Manhood Principle" that "a real man expects the greater reward" by focusing on the phrases "the joy set before him" (12:2) and "looking to the reward" (11:26). According to Lewis, real men are to follow the example set by Jesus, "the truly authentic man" who "embraced His responsibilities—a *will* to obey, a *work* to do, and a *woman* to love" (i.e., the church).[42] Apart from the question of whether the goal of the author of Hebrews is to present Jesus as the model husband-father, which it clearly is not, Lewis's understanding of joy and reward is the opposite of what Hebrews 11–12 emphasizes. Lewis explicitly lists the "great gains and rewards" of his "own quest for authentic manhood": a good reputation, the admiration of his wife, four well-adjusted children, the respect of other men, innumerable divine blessings, and "a growing satisfaction about my life."[43]

In Hebrews 11, to the contrary, the consistent emphasis is on the *heavenly*, not the *earthly*, reward, since they "did not receive the things promised" (11:13, cf. v. 39), some of the faithful suffering persecution, imprisonment, and even martyrdom (vv. 35–37). And Jesus, of course, also neither sought nor experienced an earthly reward. After enduring the shame and pain of the cross, Jesus "sat down at the right hand of the throne of God," his joy-bringing heavenly reward (Heb. 12:2). Furthermore, Lewis's use of this text completely ignores the occasion of the epistle to the Hebrews, which is usually understood as addressing Jewish Christians. Like the Old Testament faithful described in Hebrews 11, they have suffered persecution, public insult, and imprisonment (10:32–34) and are tempted to abandon the faith. So the author admonishes them, "So do not throw away your confidence; it will be richly rewarded. You need to persevere so that when you have done the will of God, you will receive what he has promised. For, 'In just a little while, he who is coming will come and will not delay'" (Heb. 10:35–37). Like the Old Testament faithful and like Jesus, they are urged to endure hardship in hope of joyfully receiving an eternal reward at Jesus's second coming. By neglecting the situation of the first-century readers of Hebrews, Lewis misuses the text, seeking to persuade men to pursue "authentic manhood" with the prospect of earthly rewards.

Joel Osteen offers a similar example in which he substitutes the promise of earthly reward for an originally spiritual and primarily heavenly reward in his use of Ephesians 2:6–7. These verses describe the lofty position of Christians: "And God raised us up with Christ and seated us with him in the heavenly realms in Christ Jesus, in order that in the coming ages he might show the incomparable riches of his grace, expressed in his kindness to us in Christ Jesus." Paul writes this letter to explain God's grand purpose for the church—"to bring unity to all things in heaven and on earth under Christ" by reconciling believers to God and to each other (Eph. 1:10)—to Christians in Ephesus. Osteen, however, understands the promise in Ephesians 2:7 of God's "far and beyond favor" (his paraphrase) as his desire "to increase you financially, by giving you promotions, fresh ideas, and creativity," which depends on us first abandoning our "small-minded thinking."[44] This could hardly be more remote from the letter's original occasion.

What led Paul to write 1 Corinthians? The church at Corinth was plagued by both internal divisions and sexual immorality (1 Cor. 5:1–2, 11). Paul seeks to combat the latter by reminding them that the body "is not meant for sexual immorality but for the Lord, and the Lord for the body" (1 Cor. 6:13). Since our bodies are "temples of the Holy Spirit," we should "honor God" with them (vv. 19–20) by not uniting "the members of Christ . . . with a prostitute" (v. 15). Larry Mercer, however, sees in this text not a call to "flee from sexual immorality" (v. 18) but rather a challenge to help our children to "establish healthy habits early," including regular exercise and a vegetable-rich diet.[45] But Paul is concerned here with blatant sin (i.e., tolerated incest), not merely with poor eating habits! These examples illustrate the need to take seriously the original situation that prompted the writing of the individual New Testament letters before applying them to ourselves, asking ourselves whether our situation today is sufficiently close to the situation of their first-century readers.

In this chapter we have not examined all of the literary genres found in the Bible. We have not discussed the Gospels or the parables of Jesus. We also could have considered the main types of psalms, such as laments, hymns, and thanksgiving psalms, or the unique challenges posed by the apocalyptic features of the book of Revelation. There are helpful introductions to biblical interpretation that give detailed attention to each of these literary categories. We hope that we have demonstrated, however, that the key features of each biblical genre must be understood and taken into consideration when we seek to interpret and apply them. Otherwise, not only will we fail to enjoy the rich diversity of the biblical menu, but we may also misuse these texts as a result.

Think about It

1. Why do you think Bible readers often fail to distinguish between the various literary genres found in the Bible when they are careful to distinguish between modern genres such as personal letters, news magazines, and legal contracts? How would giving more attention to these distinctions change the way you view Scripture?

2. According to Acts 2:42–47, the earliest believers in Jesus Christ "devoted themselves to the apostles' teaching and to fellowship, to the breaking of bread and to prayer. Everyone was filled with awe at the many wonders and signs performed by the apostles. All the believers were together and had everything in common. They sold property and possessions to give to anyone who had need. Every day they continued to meet together in the temple courts. They broke bread in their homes and ate together with glad and sincere hearts, praising God and enjoying the favor of all the people. And the Lord added to their number daily those who were being saved." How do we decide which of these actions and results were merely true of the early church and which of them should be true of every church?

Read about It

1. The best introductory guide to the genres of the Bible is Gordon D. Fee and Douglas Stuart, *How to Read the Bible for*

All Its Worth, 3rd ed. (Grand Rapids: Zondervan, 2003). The authors offer basic guidelines for interpreting and properly applying ten genres—from the Old Testament: the narratives, the laws, the prophets, the psalms, and wisdom; from the New Testament: the epistles, Acts, the Gospels, the parables, and Revelation. They give helpful interpretive insights into many biblical texts as illustrations and list common mistakes to avoid. Most basic introductions to interpreting the Bible also include several chapters on the special problems posed by various literary genres.

2. John and Kim Walton, in *The Bible Story Handbook: A Resource for Teaching 175 Stories from the Bible* (Wheaton: Crossway, 2010), have coauthored a helpful guide for teaching the narratives of the Old Testament and New Testament. For each story they offer a lesson focus and lesson applications, and they summarize the biblical context, interpretive issues in the story, important background information, and mistakes to avoid.

6

Caution—Prooftexting in Progress

Avoiding Pitfalls in Application

You can find a Bible verse to support anything if you look long enough, especially if you check out a number of different English translations. Consider Philippians 3:2 in the NKJV, which warns: "Beware of dogs." (The ESV and NASB are similar.) It is a perfect Bible verse to post on the backyard fence that encloses your pet Rottweilers, if you are so inclined. Of course, the context of Philippians 3 makes it clear that Paul is not referring to furry four-legged creatures but rather to promoters of Judaism (often called "Judaizers") who could lead the believers in Philippi astray. This is just a fun example, but it illustrates how we automatically turn to the Bible for support, whatever the occasion. I was reminded of this when reading an article in *World*, a Christian news magazine. The article's author claims: "Scratch a good secular saying and you'll find a Bible verse underneath."[1] The author then proceeds to seek a Bible source for the saying "Ninety percent of life is just showing up." In the course of wandering about in the Bible, he offers illustrations such as "Jesus showed up, and so you are saved." But surely Jesus did much more than just show up!

One of the common practices of Rick Warren in his bestselling books is quoting from a wide range of Bible translations. In *The Purpose Driven Life* he cites fifteen different English versions in nearly a thousand Scripture quotations. In an appendix, "Why Use So Many Translations?," he explains why. He varies translations in order to bring out "nuances and shades of meaning" that other translations miss and to help the reader see "God's truth in new, *fresh* ways, especially with familiar verses." Furthermore, rather than quoting an entire verse, he frequently "focused on the phrase that was appropriate"—just like Jesus and the apostles who "often just quoted a phrase to make a point."[2]

Warren's reasons may be valid to a degree, and he certainly could not be expected to quote a thousand biblical verses in full and discuss their literary contexts. The problem is that his use of loose paraphrases, carefully selected translations, and brief textual snippets allows him at times to make spiritual points that are not supported by the verse *in its entirety, understood in context*. A case in point is his "purpose-driven" emphasis, which he develops from various verses that use the word "purpose"—1 Corinthians 2:7; Ephesians 1:11–12; Colossians 1:16 (all from the Message); and Psalm 138:8 (NIV 1984).[3] Warren, using Isaiah 49:4, also contrasts "the benefits of purpose-driven living" with a person who lacks purpose: "Without God, life has no purpose, and without purpose, life has no meaning. Without meaning, life has no significance or hope. In the Bible, many different people have expressed this hopelessness. Isaiah complained, 'I have labored to no purpose; I have spent my strength in vain and for nothing.'"[4]

The problem with Warren's use of Isaiah 49:4 becomes clear when we read the entire verse in its context and consider its use in the New Testament:

> Listen to me, you islands;
>   hear this, you distant nations:
> Before I was born the LORD called me;
>   from my mother's womb he has spoken my name.
> He made my mouth like a sharpened sword,
>   in the shadow of his hand he hid me;
> he made me into a polished arrow
>   and concealed me in his quiver.
> He said to me, "You are my servant,
>   Israel, in whom I will display my splendor."

> But I said, "*I have labored in vain;*
> *I have spent my strength for nothing at all.*
> Yet what is due me is in the LORD's hand,
> and my reward is with my God." (Isa. 49:1–4, emphasis
> added)

In this passage it is unlikely that the prophet Isaiah is complaining about his own personal situation since he is addressed as "my servant, Israel" in verse 3. It is possible that the speaker is a representative Israelite speaking on behalf of the nation as a whole. Christian interpreters have traditionally understood this text as describing God's supreme servant, Jesus Christ, partly due to the reuse of the "mouth like a sharpened sword" simile from Isaiah 49:2 in Revelation 1:16; 2:12; and 2:16.[5] If this interpretation is correct—that Isaiah 49:4 prophetically presents words of Jesus—then it is certainly ironic that Warren uses them to portray the purposeless life! Regardless of how we identify the speaker, the context makes it clear that this person is not experiencing a life lacking in purpose: divinely called before birth (49:1), divinely equipped for effective speech (49:2), divinely protected (49:2), destined to glorify God (49:3), and confident that he will ultimately receive a divine reward even though his labor seems to be unproductive (49:4).

Much popular use of the Bible is similar to this example from Rick Warren. Verses or phrases from verses are used liberally (or references listed) to support or illustrate the author's point without giving any attention to what the text as a whole is actually communicating. Perhaps it would be helpful to post a warning sign on certain books and religious websites: Caution—prooftexting in progress! "Prooftexting" is a general and well-known label for using a biblical text for a purpose contrary to its original intention. But there are a number of different mistakes that we can make in applying a biblical text to a modern situation.

Reading Biblical Texts: A Two-Step Process

Christian hermeneutics (the study of the principles and methods used to understand texts) typically conceives of interpretation as a two-step process, often distinguishing between what the biblical text *meant* originally and what it *means* today. This is based on the realization that the biblical world and the modern (especially Western) world are literally "worlds apart." They are separated by differences in language, culture, values, and circumstances. In order to understand the Bible properly today, we first need to journey back to this ancient world, seeking as best we can to hear the Scriptures through the ears of their first readers. Then we are prepared to carry the message of Scripture back to our world.[6]

In the previous three chapters, our primary focus has been on the first step. We have discussed ways biblical texts are misinterpreted due to ignoring their context, mistaking the meanings of specific words, and overlooking how a text's literary genre affects or even determines its meaning. In this chapter we will turn to the second step and examine potential pitfalls in applying biblical texts to our world. Our effort to connect the biblical world with our own often requires extensive reflection so that we do not construct inadequate bridges between them.

Actually, it is misleading to suggest that a biblical text had one meaning in the seventh century BC and now has a different meaning in the twenty-first century AD. Although a text may take on new depth when read in the light of the Bible as a whole and of the two-millennia history of the Christian church, the modern meaning should echo the ancient meaning. We believe that from the time God first inspired biblical authors to write the individual books of Holy Scripture, he intended for these books to address multiple generations of his people. This is why he led his people to preserve and gather them into an authoritative collection of individual books. Even though these texts reflect the culture in which they were written, they communicate a message from God that transcends that ancient culture.

What we are concerned with here is how our contemporary *application* of a biblical text may differ from that of an ancient believer, even though its *meaning* has not really changed. To offer a clear example, Leviticus 1–7 describes the various offerings and sacrifices that the Israelites were required to present to God. Based on the conviction that "all Scripture is God-breathed and is useful for teaching, rebuking, correcting and training in righteousness" (2 Tim. 3:16), the interpreter asks: How am I to respond to these detailed instructions? There are a number of possible responses:

1. Those regulations were certainly complicated—and animal sacrifices are expensive. I'm glad we don't have to follow them anymore as Christians!

2. Since the Bible is God's Word, I've decided that I have to sacrifice a sheep in the church parking lot. Why is that policeman heading toward me?

3. My pastor speaks again and again about "sacrificial giving," so I guess the check I put in the offering plate on Sunday is my Christian sacrifice.

4. The Old Testament describes a number of different sacrifices to bring, depending on the circumstances. Maybe by learning more about them, I can learn something from them about how to maintain and celebrate my own relationship with God.

Applying a biblical text today involves identifying an obedient response appropriate to our own situation that corresponds to the purpose of the ancient text. To do so, it is helpful to distinguish between the two steps of interpretation and application, but two-stepping can lead to missteps until you have mastered the hermeneutical dance. These two steps are closely related. In many of the examples cited in the preceding three chapters, it would have been difficult to distinguish between errors of interpretation and errors of application. Both kinds of errors are often found together since misinterpretation frequently leads to misapplication. Yet it is possible to correctly apply a text that has been interpreted incorrectly. A Bible reader, for example, could misunderstand the repeated exhortation in 1 John to "love one another" (3:11, 23; 4:7, 11) as a call to love everybody we meet (too broad) rather than understanding that the phrase "one another" normally refers only to relationships within the church (narrower; see Rom. 14:13; 15:14; 1 Cor. 1:10; 16:20; 2 Cor. 13:11; Gal. 5:13; 2 Thess. 1:3; Heb. 13:1; James 4:11; 5:9 in which the readers are addressed as "brothers and sisters"). But if that same reader recently had a falling out with a member of her small group at church, she might be convicted to apply these particular verses exclusively to her relationship with other believers, which would be correct. To apply these verses well, we would still need to reflect on how we appropriately express love within the church today in ways that might differ from expected expressions of Christian love in first-century Ephesus.

Of course, it is also possible to interpret a text correctly and still misapply it. For example, the reader of Ephesians 5:18 ("Do not get drunk on wine, which leads to debauchery. Instead, be filled with the Spirit") might correctly note the surprising contrast made in the verse between wine and the Spirit. He might also observe the parallel between being full of either wine or the Spirit—a correct interpretation. But then he might misapply the text by promoting an alcohol-free lifestyle and a passionate pursuit of publicly displayed charismatic gifts.

In this chapter, I will discuss and illustrate the major ways in which the hermeneutical traveler can get lost on the way from the biblical world to the modern world. We will discover in the process that determining how to apply an ancient divine word *to them* as a contemporary divine word *to us* is more complex than it at first appears. I will conclude the chapter by offering some basic guidelines for properly applying biblical texts, also illustrating them with several published examples.

Pitfalls in Application

Let us examine six common forms of misapplication of biblical texts: insufficiently analogous situations, anachronism, psychologizing, unwarranted generalization, privatizing corporate contexts, and spiritualizing.

Insufficiently Analogous Situations

Christians reading the Bible today may have two simultaneous responses: (1) God is speaking directly to me in this text. (2) The world of the Bible is very different than my world today. As a result, they may apply a text to their own personal situations by making weak or questionable connections to the text's original setting. One textbook on biblical interpretation refers to these as "insufficiently analogous situations." The reader may "correctly interpret passages in their literary and historical contexts but then bring them to bear on situations where they simply do not apply."[7]

Consider the following familiar list of application questions:

1. Is there a command for us to obey?
2. Is there a promise for us to claim?
3. Is there an example for us to follow?
4. Is there a sin for us to avoid or confess?
5. Is there a reason for us to give thanksgiving or praise?[8]

The fourth and fifth questions are not too problematic. The first two, however, may lead to applications that involve insufficiently analogous situations if the command or promise concerns only a limited group or situation and so should not be generalized as applying to all believers.[9] And finally, the third question can lead to an unwarranted call to imitate the behavior of a flawed biblical figure whose words or actions are not intended to be taken as a model.

In *Disciplines of the Beautiful Woman* Anne Ortlund assures the beginning Bible student that no instruction is needed due to the work of the Holy Spirit. "If you say you don't know how to study the Bible, don't worry. Just start in! That's why God has given his Holy Spirit, to teach you. Amazing what 1 John 2:27 says: 'You have no need for anyone to teach you; but . . . His anointing teaches you about all things'" (NASB). If this is what John had in mind when he wrote this verse, then there is no reason for me to write a book like this since beginning Bible readers who have the Holy Spirit are not in need of any further instruction. Ironically, though, Ortlund explains that her preacher husband benefited greatly from good teachers and the study books they recommended to him.[10]

The question is whether a beginning Bible student today is in an analogous situation to the readers of 1 John. First of all, John's readers did not have the New Testament to study like modern believers. They were largely dependent on the apostle John and other traveling Christian teachers, some of whom were the false teachers John's letter warns against. John refers to them in the preceding verse: "I am writing these things to you about those who are trying to lead you astray" (1 John 2:26). He then refers to "the anointing" that these believers have received, presumably from the Holy Spirit. This anointing serves to keep them from being deceived by these false teachers, a specific danger to which Ortlund does not refer.

Second, the surrounding verses clearly indicate that John's readers still rely on human teachers. A few verses earlier John writes: "As for you, see that what you have heard from the beginning remains in you" (v. 24). They did not hear the gospel directly from Jesus himself. Instead, they heard it from apostolic eyewitnesses like John, who assures them, "That which was from the beginning, which we have heard, which we have seen with our eyes, which we have looked at and our hands have touched—this we proclaim concerning the Word of life" (1 John 1:1). And John is writing this letter to them because they are still in need of his instruction. In sum, John is assuring his readers in 1 John 2:27 that the Holy Spirit will help them to hold fast to the truth that they already understand and believe, rather than being seduced by the false teachers. He is not promising them that the Spirit will prevent them from misinterpreting the Bible in their efforts to increase their knowledge of God's truth. Accordingly, this verse in 1 John should not be applied to the process of biblical interpretation. Nevertheless, Bible readers today may be in a similar situation as John's first-century readers when a cult member rings their doorbell. Today the same Spirit "anointing" can help reassure us that we are "in the truth" and protect us from being persuaded by their arguments.

As the earliest biblical statement about marriage, Genesis 2:24 is foundational to many Christian marriage books. A familiar three-step process is derived from the KJV translation ("Therefore shall a man leave his father and his mother, and shall cleave unto his wife: and they shall be one flesh"): leaving, cleaving (they rhyme!), and becoming one flesh. I must confess that I used these three "steps," as well, the first time I did premarital counseling for an engaged couple. The use of the verb "shall" in the KJV may also remind readers of the wording in the Ten Commandments, wrongly leading them to view this as an exhortation or instruction rather than an observation. They conclude, therefore, that we should prepare for marriage today just like the first readers of Genesis—perhaps even like Adam and Eve did. In a chapter with the title "Are You Both Ready for Marriage?," Blaine Smith uses this questionable approach to the verse. He advises that it is "normally unwise to marry before each has lived at a full responsibility level independent of parents for at least two years," citing Genesis 2:24 as the basis for his statement.[11] This may be good advice today when some speak of a general "failure to launch" as twentysomethings delay their departure from the parental nest, preferring its comfort and security to the challenges and freedoms of life outside, but it is a poor application of the message of Genesis 2:24.

Those anticipating marriage today are in a very different situation from those described by Genesis 2:24. First of all, this verse does not describe Adam's situation since he had no parents to leave! Instead, looking back on centuries of marriage, the author Moses observes: "That is why a man leaves his father and mother and is united to his wife, and they become one flesh." Furthermore, this verse does not refer to a man moving away from his parents to live elsewhere. A man in ancient Israel certainly would never consider leaving his parents' home for two years prior to marriage in order to get ready! According to Old Testament scholar John Walton, ancient Near Eastern sources indicate that the wife was actually the one who physically left her family to become part of her husband's tribe, and the new couple tended to live as a part of the husband's extended family in a family compound. For the first few months of the marriage, however, she may have continued to live with her parents, probably until she conceived.[12]

Therefore, this verse should be understood as indicating the need for a new *loyalty* rather than a new *location*. The man is drawn away emotionally from his parents toward his wife because they are in fact *one* flesh by virtue of Eve being created from Adam (Gen. 2:23). When this verse is quoted in the New Testament (Matt. 19:5; Mark 10:7; Eph. 5:31), the emphasis is similarly on the permanence of the union, not the physical leaving of parents. In applying Genesis 2:24 to the problems of youthful immaturity and irresponsibility today, Smith fails to acknowledge that this was certainly not the situation being addressed in this chapter of the Genesis creation account. In any case, this verse is *describing* the nature of the marital relationship rather than *prescribing* the way it should be.

The two preceding examples illustrate the problem with assuming that we are in a similar situation as those directly addressed or described by a biblical text. In dealing with Old Testament texts, we must always consider whether or not they involve commands or promises restricted to the Israelites as God's chosen nation under the Sinai and Davidic covenants. This raises a question, for instance, regarding whether the common application of 2 Chronicles 7:14 to the corporate well-being of the United States is appropriate: "If my people, who are called by my name, will humble themselves and pray and seek my face and turn from their wicked ways, then I will hear from heaven, and I will forgive their sin and will heal their land."

According to *The American Patriot's Bible*, both Dwight D. Eisenhower (1953) and Ronald Reagan (1981 and 1985) placed their hands on 2 Chronicles 7:14 as they took the presidential oath of office.[13] Stan Huberfeld devotes an entire book entitled *2 Chronicles 7:14 Revival* to the implications of this verse for the United States today.[14] John Piper helpfully reminds us, however, that "when we apply this text to our contemporary situation, 'my people' would refer to the Christian Church who cannot say, in whatever country that they reside, that this country is 'their land.' The church has no land, the way Israel had a land." Piper goes on to suggest that the proper application of this text would be for the church to humble herself and pray, turning from her wicked ways in hopes that God will respond by healing *the church*. "But it goes beyond what this text assures if we say that any country where the Christian church humbles herself will experience a Great Awakening."[15]

Seeking to turn key biblical figures into "everyman" characters is a common application problem. We may wrongly assume that their unique experiences of being called and equipped by God for specific tasks in redemptive history should mirror the daily experiences of every believer. In the preceding chapter we saw the danger in treating the call of Samuel or Isaiah in this manner. Will the situation of the contemporary Christian ever be *identical* to that of the ancient Israelite following Moses through the wilderness or celebrating Passover with King Hezekiah of Judah? Or will it ever be exactly like that of the first-century Jew listening to Jesus on the shore of the Sea of Galilee or to Paul in Philippi? No, but this does not prevent us from finding appropriate ways to respond to the teaching of these texts. We will discuss some guidelines for doing this later in the chapter. In seeking "sufficiently analogous situations," it is always helpful to consider both how our situation as a contemporary Christian is *similar* to that of the person or group described or addressed by a specific biblical text and how it is *different*. We then should reflect on how these differences affect our application of the text today and *acknowledge* these differences in discussing that application.

Anachronism

A second faulty approach to application is related to the previous one. It involves imposing modern categories, labels, and institutional structures on biblical features in an effort to make the Bible address them. Lois Lebar in *Education That Is Christian* calls Christ Jesus the "Master Teacher par excellence," citing Mark 4:33; Luke 24:27; John 2:24–25; 14:6; and 16:12 in support. Jesus "perfectly embodied the truth, He perfectly understood His pupils, and He used perfect methods in order to change people."[16] A couple of older books are devoted fully to deriving educational principles from Jesus's teaching ministry.[17] Lebar acknowledges the problem of turning to Jesus's ministry to shape Christian education today: "Students of Scripture sometimes wonder how our teaching today can be compared with Christ's teaching when He never taught in a classroom and we seldom teach outside one. What difference do four walls make?"[18] She then turns to analyzing Jesus's "method" of dealing with the Samaritan woman (John 4:1–42), using it to develop principles such as making contact with the pupil, getting the pupil actively involved, and putting the truth to work.

Now, Jesus was clearly an effective teacher, although the point of comparison in the New Testament was with other Jewish rabbis, not with modern Sunday school teachers or Bible school professors. Jesus is also frequently called "Teacher" [Gk. *didaskalos*] in the Gospels (nearly fifty times). Yet to analyze Gospel narratives in an effort to demonstrate that Jesus exemplifies sound educational methods is anachronistic. Lebar, in effect, is *not* deriving lessons from Jesus the Master Teacher but rather imposing the categories of educational theory on his evangelistic dialogues. John does not describe the Samaritan woman as Jesus's "pupil" but, metaphorically speaking, as part of the ripened crop that Jesus harvests "for eternal life" (John 4:35–36).

For Frank Minirth and his three coauthors, Jesus is not the Master Teacher, the model educator. Instead he is the model Christian counselor, who "treats twelve tired men"—his disciples—helping them to avoid or recover from ministry "burnout" (citing Mark 6:30–32).[19] Significant burnout research began in the early 1980s. Psychologist Christina Maslach defines burnout as "a syndrome of emotional exhaustion, depersonalization, and reduced personal accomplishment that can occur among individuals who do 'people work' of some kind."[20] Those experiencing burnout "frequently cannot face the future, and they detach themselves from interpersonal closeness. Sensing themselves to be drained emotionally, they also suffer spiritually."[21]

Armed with a modern understanding of burnout, its causes, its symptoms, and its cures, these coauthors turn to the Scriptures, expecting them to offer some inspired guidelines for dealing with it. In their analysis, Solomon suffered from burnout (Eccles. 2:17–23), as did Moses (Num. 20) and Elijah (1 Kings 19). What about the disciples upon their return from a preaching tour of unspecified length, as described in Mark 6:30–32?

> The apostles gathered around Jesus and reported to him all they had done and taught. Then, because so many people were coming and going that they did not even have a chance to eat, he said to them, "Come with me by yourselves to a quiet place and get some rest." So they went away by themselves in a boat to a solitary place.

Since Jesus "sensed that the burnout factor was present in them," he prescribed a change in location and in activity or level of responsibility, as well as some time off. Minirth and his coauthors even speculate that shortly thereafter, when the disciples were unable to grasp the full implications of Jesus's miraculous multiplication of the bread and fish, it was the result of burnout (vv. 51–52: "They were completely amazed, for they had not understood about the loaves; their hearts were hardened").[22]

It is certainly possible that some individuals portrayed in the biblical narratives suffered from burnout, depending on how it is defined. The problem of burnout did not begin when a label was coined for it! But there is no clear indication in Mark 6 that the disciples were exhausted or harried. In fact, they may have missed only one meal (v. 31). And it is even less clear that they were emotionally drained, unable to face the future, and relationally challenged. Furthermore, the narrative goes on to relate that the disciples did not get the anticipated rest (vv. 32–33), other than a brief boat ride across the Sea of Galilee. So it would appear that their counselor was weak on his follow-through! On a more basic level, individuals in the biblical world had to devote a significant amount of time to the necessary activities of life, including meal preparation and travel. This makes it unlikely that they experienced the same levels of work-related stress that many people impose on themselves today. Though no one would discount the restorative value of a brief change of pace, task, and location, we should not interpret Mark 6 as a description of how Jesus treated his disciples for burnout symptoms.

It is understandable why Christian scholars examine the Bible to find some affirmation of the findings and claims of their academic discipline. Yet while Scripture is a sufficient basis for Christian faith and obedience, it is not a comprehensive source for understanding all human phenomena. The authority of Scripture as God's inspired Word is not enhanced by well-meaning efforts to demonstrate that it anticipates all of the later discoveries of the natural and social sciences. To assume this is to misunderstand the nature and purpose of the Bible and run the risk of forced anachronistic interpretations.

Psychologizing

A third faulty approach to application involves psychologizing, that is, reading between the lines of a text to fill in the unexpressed thoughts and motivations of biblical characters. James Houston cites Ezekiel 18:2–3, calling it "a piece of ancient near-Eastern pop psychology": "What do you people mean by quoting this proverb about the land of Israel: 'The parents eat sour grapes, and the children's teeth are set on edge'? As surely as I live, declares the Sovereign LORD, you will no longer quote this proverb in Israel." Houston understands this verse in terms of the characteristics we have inherited from our parents, such as tendencies to be judgmental and mean. And he goes on to speak of "emotional resentment and prejudice" and "the wounded feelings that our parents . . . have inflicted on us." This psychological interpretation of Ezekiel 18:2 then determines how he applies the verse: "Redemption and grace stop the flow of cause-and-effect in our parenting."[23]

In his effort to promote happy families, Houston reads emotions into Ezekiel 18:2 that are not clearly there. In the process, he apparently fails to identify the genre of the saying as proverbial in nature. The proverb is also quoted in a slightly different form in Jeremiah 31:29–30, a text that may help to clarify its meaning here: "In those days people will no longer say, 'The parents have eaten sour grapes, and the children's teeth are set on edge.' Instead, everyone will die for their own sin; whoever eats sour grapes—their own teeth will be set on edge." Interpreters have typically understood Ezekiel 18:2 as expressing the Israelites' complaint that they have been exiled to Babylon as a result of their parents' sins, not their own. Implicitly then, they would also be accusing God of unjustly punishing them. Old Testament scholar Daniel Block, however, argues against this interpretation. In his view, this saying reflects a fatalistic—not a faith-filled—attitude. Instead of trusting in God, they have resigned themselves to the unchangeable cosmic rules of cause and effect, leaving them bitter and without hope.[24] Regardless of which interpretation you prefer, the saying does not refer to the inherited vices or damaged emotions of children, evoking hostility toward their parents.

Norman Vincent Peale is well known for his emphasis on the power of positive thinking. In giving advice on how to overcome fear of other people, he highlights the role of loving others: "The top curative factor . . . is to learn to love them. 'Perfect love casts out fear' (1 John 4:18 [NASB, NKJV]). The more you develop genuine appreciation and esteem for others, the less you will feel inferior in their presence and the easier, more normal, your relationship with them will be."[25] There are several questionable assumptions here: (1) that the "fear" here is between two humans, (2) that feelings of inferiority are the basis for fear, (3) that loving others is primarily expressed through appreciating and esteeming them. Disregarding the context of this phrase within 1 John 4, Peale invalidly replaces theological explanations with psychological ones.

Peale focuses here on love's expression—love consists of an appreciation that people develop toward others. John focuses on love's source—love is first and foremost from God, whose actions toward us are motivated and marked by love. Love for one another, however, is inseparable from love for God: "We love because he first loved us. . . . Whoever does not love their brother and sister, whom they have seen, cannot love God, whom they have not seen. . . . Anyone who loves God must also love their brother and sister" (1 John 4:19–21). Peale does not explain why feelings of inferiority cause us to fear others. John speaks of the believer having "confidence on the day of judgment" (v. 17) and thus explains that "fear has to do with punishment" (v. 18). So the fear that John is speaking of here is the fear of divine judgment, which a matured love for God and other believers dispels. John calls believers to acknowledge that they are loved by the Father, who "sent his Son to be the Savior of the world" (v. 14). They may then have confidence based on their love for God, which they express by loving his children and obeying his commands. That is why our love casts out fear.

As humans, we are complex psychological beings who are motivated and tossed about by a wide range of often contrary emotions. Of course, the biblical authors and characters were no different. But there are a number of problems with a psychologizing approach to the biblical text. First of all, to do so is to elevate the importance of what the biblical authors chose *not* to mention. They do not consistently convey the inner thoughts and emotions of biblical characters, other than indirectly through their speech. They do reveal inner thoughts when it is important, however. Consider 2 Kings 5, which recounts the healing of Naaman, the leprous Syrian military commander: "But Naaman went away angry and said, 'I thought that he would surely come out to me and stand and call on the name of the LORD his God, wave his hand over the spot and cure me of my leprosy. . . .' So he turned and went off in a rage" (vv. 11–12). Verse 20 also relates the thoughts of Gehazi: "Gehazi, the servant of Elisha the man of God, said to himself, 'My master was too easy on Naaman, this Aramean, by not accepting from him what he brought. As surely as the LORD lives, I will run after him and get something from him.'" Numerous texts report the special fears, sorrows, and joys of biblical characters (for example, Matt. 19:22; 28:8; Acts 16:34; 20:37–38). If no emotions or motivations are noted, we should normally assume that this detail is not important for the proper understanding of the text.

Second, in filling in psychological details, it is likely that we will often guess wrongly how individuals might have responded to a particular situation or what might have motivated them to act in a certain way. Not only do various people respond differently to the same situation, but also some of our responses are conditioned by our culture and environment. The person who is terrified by being alone in a jungle might feel at home in a crowded city, and vice versa. When we psychologize texts in an effort to apply them to our situation, we are prone to read our own emotions and motivations into them and thereby distort our interpretation.

Unwarranted Generalization

A fourth faulty practice in application is making unwarranted generalizations. This involves taking a very specific statement or situation in Scripture and applying it broadly to all Christians without sufficient indication in the text that this is legitimate. In *Wild at Heart*, John Eldredge concludes on the basis of Exodus 15:3 that "aggression is a part of the masculine *design*." He explains his logic as follows: "We are hardwired for it [aggression]. If we believe that man is made in the image of God, then we would do well to affirm that 'the LORD is a warrior; the LORD is his name.' . . . The universal nature of this ought to have convinced us by now: The boy is a warrior; the boy is his name."[26]

There are several interpretive mistakes here, despite his claim to have discovered a universal truth. First of all, "The LORD is a warrior" is one of many metaphorical statements found in Scripture. It does not describe God's essential nature or constitute his "image" any more than statements like "the LORD is" my rock, my shepherd, my light (Pss. 18:2; 23:1; 27:1). It merely compares some of God's actions with those of a human warrior, quite appropriate when the Egyptian army is bearing down on the seemingly helpless Israelites. Nor is it obvious that "The LORD is a warrior" may be appropriately paraphrased as "The LORD is aggressive." Second, God is neither male nor female, and his image is similarly nongendered. Therefore,

Eldredge has no warrant for equating what he sees as a male-specific trait with the image of God. Finally, although biblical interpreters and theologians continue to debate precisely what the "image of God" in humans involves, none of them argues that this image includes *all* of God's attributes. Eldredge makes a similar error later in the same book when he quotes Isaiah 62:5b ("as a bridegroom rejoices over his bride, so will your God rejoice over you"), remarking, "God is a romantic at heart, and he has his own bride to fight for." The logic that, since God is a Braveheart figure, every male image-bearer should be too is problematic at best.[27] (An additional concern here is that, in an age of bullying, Eldredge fails to offer a clear definition of aggression and its proper limits.)

Pastor Mark Buchanan also generalizes in an explicit but questionable manner in a brief article "Stuck on the Road to Emmaus." The article addresses the common experience of many Christians "who want to have a deeper, richer experience with Christ, but they find themselves instead whiling away their days. . . . They don't feel fulfilled."[28] Buchanan summarizes the story of the two apostles who encounter Jesus while traveling to Emmaus shortly after Jesus's resurrection in Luke 24:13–35. He focuses on verse 32: "They asked each other, 'Were not our hearts burning within us while he talked with us on the road and opened the Scriptures to us?'" Then he remarks regarding these two disciples: "their hearts are slow and burning. They are, I think, Everyman."

Buchanan bases this claim, in part, on the fact that we know so little about these two individuals (merely the name of one of them): "these two are mere silhouettes. We see them in dark outline, devoid of feature." He then concludes his meditation on this text: "Their yearning was . . . a homing device in the heart, drawing them on no matter how long the road, no matter that the 'day is almost over' (v. 29), no matter that their hearts are slow with doubt and broken with grief. Even then—especially then—their hearts still burn, and they know this journey is a good one, leading Somewhere. And it's never taken alone."[29] The biblical narratives describe the faith journeys of many individuals, and each of them may mirror our own Christian experience in some way. As such, they can encourage us to trust that the God of the Bible will prove as faithful in our situations as he was in the events portrayed in Scripture.

But it is one thing to confess that "Jesus Christ is the same yesterday and today and forever" (Heb. 13:8) and quite another to equate ourselves with these biblical characters because of "heart burn" (a metaphorical expression found only in Luke 24:32). Luke 24 as a whole emphasizes the certainty of Jesus's resurrection from the dead and the struggle of his followers to understand and believe (vv. 4, 11, 12, 24–25, 37–38, 41, 52–53) what they have seen and heard. When Jesus teaches the two disciples about the fulfillment of the Hebrew Scriptures (vv. 25–27), this clearly parallels and anticipates his instruction to the eleven (vv. 44–48). The apostles and other early followers of Jesus were involved in a unique week of redemptive history. The two disciples' "resurrection day" confusion and disappointment—"but we had hoped that he was the one who was going to redeem Israel. And what is more, it is the third day since all this took place" (v. 21)—is an experience that no modern disciple shares. In this respect, Cleopas and his unnamed traveling companion are anything but Christian "Everyman" figures.

As we seek to apply Scripture to our lives, we will naturally generalize the direct teachings of the biblical texts as well as the indirect principles they illustrate. In the process we will begin with the specific individuals and situations described in the text and then move to our situation today. As we do so, however, we need to consider whether the text warrants this kind of generalization. In some cases, the characteristics of the genre may provide a warrant. For example, proverbial sayings seek to express universal truths that reflect the human condition and not simply one particular culture. In other cases, what a narrative text illustrates indirectly is expressed directly in another text. Therefore, that text offers a warrant for generalizing the principle that is illustrated by the narrative. And finally, a warrant may be found by closely analyzing a text to distinguish between its central emphasis or message, which may be generalized, and its specific supporting details, which should not.[30]

Privatizing Corporate Contexts

A fifth problematic approach to application is treating corporate or group contexts as private or personal. This approach is the reverse of the preceding one. It involves applying to a private individual what the text addresses to a distinct group—such as the nation of Israel or a subgroup within the nation or a local New Testament church. As a modern example, consider a local banker who promised to give a generous loan to any area church undertaking a major building project. Individuals within the church, however, assumed that the promise also applied to their need for a bank loan to finance a home renovation project.

We already discussed an example of this in chapter 5 in connection with Jeremiah 29:11: "'For I know the plans I have for you,' declares the LORD, 'plans to prosper you and not to harm you, plans to give you hope and a future.'" This verse is addressed to former citizens of Judah exiled to Babylon. The "you" in this verse is a plural, not a singular, and the promises apply to the nation in exile as a whole. According to Rick Warren, however, Jeremiah 29:11 promises the reader that "wonderful changes are going to happen in your life as soon as you begin to live it on purpose."[31] He follows this verse with Ephesians 3:20 from the Living Bible ("God . . . is able to do far more than we would ever dare to ask or even dream of—infinitely beyond our highest prayers, desires, thoughts, or hopes"). And he introduces it with the comment: "You may feel that you are facing an impossible situation, but the Bible says . . ."[32] In this case, the specific contents of Ephesians 3:20 (which refers to our "desires, thoughts, or hopes"; NIV: "all we ask or imagine") and the surrounding context (for example, the prayer that "Christ may dwell in your hearts through faith" in v. 17) both indicate that the promise is being extended to individual believers, not just the Ephesian church as a whole. Therefore, Warren's use of this verse is more appropriate.

Loren Cunningham, the founder of Youth With A Mission, offers twelve basic points on "Hearing the Voice of God," which he calls "a basic right of every child of God." His second point is "Allow God to speak to you in the *way* He chooses," and he cites the call of Samuel in 1 Samuel 3:9 as an illustration. After correctly noting that God may choose to speak to us through his Word, an audible voice, dreams, or visions, he concludes: "But probably the most common of all means is through the quiet, *inner voice* (Isaiah 30:21)."[33] This verse does not obviously refer to an *inner* voice: "Whether you turn to the right or to the left, your ears will hear a voice behind you, saying, 'This is the way; walk in it.'" Taken by itself, that may be a logical inference since today we probably do not expect to hear God speak out loud to us. Verse 20 identifies the voice as belonging either to the Teacher (that is, God; ESV, HCSB, NASB, NRSV) or (human) teachers (so NET, NIV, NKJV) whom the people will see with their own eyes. If the latter translation is correct, then this verse is not referring to an inner voice.

But the immediate context in Isaiah 30 also clearly identifies a very specific recipient and situation for this prophetic promise. Because of their rebellion and sin (v. 9), the inhabitants of Jerusalem have been afflicted by God through a military attack, presumably by the Assyrians (vv. 16–17). They have relied in vain on assistance from the Egyptians (v. 3) and rejected divine instruction through the prophets (vv. 9–10). But in the future they will once again repent (v. 15) and call on God for help (v. 19), rejecting their false gods (v. 22). Then their land will experience renewed fertility according to the provisions of the Sinai covenant (v. 23), and God will heal them (v. 26), delivering them from Assyria's power (v. 31). More important, the prophet addresses the "people" here as a corporate entity (vv. 9, 19, 26), not as individuals. Given all of this descriptive detail, it is clear that this biblical promise cannot be so easily generalized. Therefore, it is questionable practice to use this promise as the single text to illustrate Cunningham's claim that God most commonly guides individual believers through the "inner voice."

We are conditioned by modern Western society to think primarily in terms of the individual, of our own personal needs and interests. And this type of thinking permeates the church as well. Thus we tend to assume that everything the Bible affirms or promises is directed to us as individual believers. But both the Old Testament and the New Testament are primarily directed to God's people (Israel or the church) as a whole. Therefore, when we appropriate corporate statements to ourselves as individuals, we need to justify it. In many texts, such as in the example of Isaiah 30 just discussed, we are on firmer ground if we keep our focus on God's character and his dealings with Israel. That passage should encourage us that our trust is in the same God who assured the inhabitants of Jerusalem so many centuries ago: "Yet the LORD longs to be gracious to you; therefore he will rise up to show you compassion. For the LORD is a God of justice. Blessed are all who wait for him!" (Isa. 30:18).

Spiritualizing

The final common form of misapplication we will discuss involves spiritualizing biblical texts, especially narratives, finding a spiritual message in nearly every detail. This approach makes liberal use of typology and allegory as interpretive methods, and it often tends to find Jesus on every page of Scripture. Those who practice this approach justify it from the Bible. A clear example of this is found in Dr. Bill Hamon's introduction to a book by Sandie Freed:

> Most theologians declare that everything that happened in the natural in the Old Testament is a type and shadow of what takes place spiritually in the New Testament Church. The book of Hebrews uses the tabernacle of Moses with all its furniture, functions, sacrifices and offerings to explain Jesus and His Church. The apostle Paul declared this to be a proper hermeneutical practice in Romans 15:4 and 1 Corinthians 10:6, 11.[34]

The use of the word "everything" in the first sentence implies that every single event that is recorded in the Old Testament happened and has meaning for us today because it prefigures New Testament realities. This could suggest that the Old Testament texts had little meaning—even no divinely revealed message—for the people of God prior to the coming of Jesus.

But even the book of Hebrews makes no such global claim. It focuses on key Old Testament individuals and events and on key features of the Old Testament sacrificial system. It never suggests that every tent peg of the tabernacle helped to "explain Jesus and His Church." Romans 15:4 ("For everything that was written in the past was written to teach us, so that through the endurance taught in the Scriptures and the encouragement they provide we might have hope") does not support Hamon's claim that we should interpret everything in the Old Testament as a "type and shadow" of the New Testament. In Romans 15:4 Paul is explaining why he has just quoted the Old Testament (from Ps. 69:9) in the preceding verse to illustrate how Jesus chose not to please himself: "The insults of those who insult you [that is, God] have fallen on me [in Paul's application, Jesus]." This should motivate "strong" believers in Rome to do the same (vv. 1–2). Although Psalm 69 is commonly understood as pointing to the future sufferings of Christ (compare Ps. 69:9 with John 2:17; Ps. 69:21 with John 19:28–29; and Ps. 69:25 with Acts 1:16–20), Paul's point here is much broader. The endurance modeled by Old Testament believers should be a rich source of encouragement and hope for Christians. The thrust of 1 Corinthians 10:11 (and 10:6) is similarly restrained: "These things happened to them as examples and were written down as warnings for us, on whom the culmination of the ages has come."

Convinced that this approach is correct, Sandie Freed offers a rather extreme example of spiritualizing in her effort to expose the devil's many weapons. In discussing Genesis 14, which recounts Abraham's liberation of Lot and his family when they were captured by four enemy kings, Freed claims, "By following the steps Abram took to free his family from slavery, we can release our loved ones from demonic captivity." Her primary interpretive technique here is to offer unsubstantiated etymologies of the names of the key characters in the narrative and then to derive spiritual truths from them, as follows:[35]

Abraham the Hebrew ("one who crosses over")—our example of crossing over any rivers of doubt that God will save our families from death and despair

Chedorlaomer ("binding up")—this demonic spirit imprisons or binds us so that we cannot move forward

Tidal ("terrible, to make afraid")—this spirit produces fear in us so that we shrink back from warfare

Amraphel ("sayer of darkness")—this spirit promotes doubt in us in every situation

Arioch ("lion-like")—this spirit roars like a lion, attempting to kill and destroy us

Freed transforms a historical narrative recounting Abraham's bold and successful rescue of his nephew from foreign kings into an exorcism of four demons, importing *her* message into the text. In its context Genesis 14 serves to illustrate how Abram blessed the king of Sodom, was blessed by Melchizedek, the king of Salem, and trusted in God rather than in conquest to make him rich. This purpose completely disappears in Freed's interpretation.

Thoughts on Proper Application

In the preceding pages I have sought to identify the most prominent flawed approaches to biblical application that are used in popular Christian writing. This raises the question of how we should properly apply the ancient biblical text to the contemporary church. It is actually easier to point out when a text has been incorrectly applied than to identify and defend its correct application(s). Entire books have been written on this subject in recent decades without producing a consensus. Our goal here is to focus our application on the primary message of the text, in the process taking into consideration the text's multiple contexts, as discussed in chapter 3.

A dominant approach in evangelical interpretation has been to identify and apply the key principle implied by the text. Old Testament scholar Walter Kaiser Jr. explains this approach: "To 'principlize' is to [re]state the author's propositions, arguments, narrations, and illustrations in timeless abiding truths with special focus on the application of those truths to the current needs of the church."[36] We identify the key principle by giving particular attention to the subject, emphasis, structure, and development of thought in a particular text. Paul appears to use this approach in 1 Corinthians 9:7–12 and 1 Timothy 5:17–18 when he quotes Deuteronomy 25:4 ("Do not muzzle an ox while it is treading out the grain"). Somewhat surprisingly, he uses this agricultural law to justify financially supporting the ministries of missionaries and pastors. His application of this law does not involve spiritualizing the ox and the grain but identifying the principle underlying the law: "whoever plows and threshes should be able to do so in the hope of sharing in the harvest" (1 Cor. 9:10)—that is, a worker's work should be rewarded.

Recently, the exclusive use of principles in application has been criticized. Interpreters who seek to derive timeless principles from culturally conditioned ancient texts sometimes fail to recognize how much their own judgments are culturally conditioned rather than universal. Interaction with interpreters from other parts of the world has revealed—sometimes painfully so—how much the core values of Western interpreters can differ from those in the global South. Furthermore, sometimes biblical principles can take on an authority that overshadows that of the inspired biblical text. God did not choose to reveal himself to us in a list of principles but rather in a rich collection of various kinds of texts. It is the Scriptures themselves with all their distinctive genre features and stylistic details that are inspired and "useful for teaching, rebuking, correcting and training in righteousness" (2 Tim. 3:16).

These critiques have led to a greater emphasis on immersing ourselves in Scripture as a whole rather than focusing on applying individual texts. We should first seek to gain a strategic understanding of the dramatic sweep of salvation history and to familiarize ourselves with God's character and purposes for his people in the world. This will help us acquire the wisdom to act "biblically" as we encounter new questions, challenges, and situations not directly addressed by the Bible. Rather than seeking to locate a specific verse that addresses our concerns—or forcing it to do so—we can understand our situation in light of Scripture as a whole. Like any acquired skill, proper interpretation and application grow easier with practice. Our best efforts should also be accompanied by prayer as we depend on the Holy Spirit to guide us and to protect us from carelessly or intentionally misusing God's Word.

Think about It

1. The next time you hear a sermon in your local church, listen carefully to how the speaker applies the biblical text. Does the application flow directly from the primary emphasis and message of the text, or is it based on secondary details?

2. Examine how various New Testament authors use sayings from the Old Testament book of Proverbs. Here is a list of some key passages:

Old Testament	New Testament
Proverbs 11:31	1 Peter 4:18
Proverbs 3:11–12	Hebrews 12:5–6
Proverbs 3:34	James 4:6; 1 Peter 5:5
Proverbs 10:12	James 5:20; 1 Peter 4:8
Proverbs 22:8	2 Corinthians 9:6–7
Proverbs 24:12	Matthew 16:27; Romans 2:6
Proverbs 25:21–22	Romans 12:20
Proverbs 26:11	2 Peter 2:22

What can you learn from this analysis about how New Testament authors applied this Old Testament genre to their concerns?

3. In *God Isn't in a Hurry*, Warren Wiersbe writes:

Husbands and wives with marital problems, fathers and mothers with family problems, and individuals with deep personal problems all have a tendency to look for shortcuts; and the shortcuts only make the problem worse. . . . A shortcut solution to a problem may alter the symptoms, but it can never deal with the causes. Like the false prophets in Jeremiah's day, these "quick counselors" heal people's hurts only slightly, "saying, 'Peace, peace!' when there is no peace" (Jer. 6:14).[37]

Do you think this application involves a proper interpretation of Jeremiah 6:14 as a sufficiently analogous situation? Explain your answer.

Read about It

1. In recent decades, Christian publishers have become more aware of the fact that many biblical commentaries do an excellent job of interpreting the text but offer little help in applying it. As a result, a number of new commentary series give special attention to the question of application. One of the best of these is the NIV Application Commentary published by Zondervan. Each text is discussed under three headings: Original Meaning, Bridging Contexts, and Contemporary Significance. The second section reflects hermeneutically on issues related to properly applying the ancient text, while the third section offers specific contemporary applications.

2. Jack Kuhatschek, who previously served as the in-house editor for the NIV Application Commentary, offers a helpful how-to guide to application in *Taking the Guesswork out of Applying the Bible* (Downers Grove, IL: InterVarsity, 1990).

3. In Gary T. Meadors, ed., *Four Views on Moving Beyond the Bible to Theology* (Grand Rapids: Zondervan, 2009), four prominent scholars present their own approach to applying the Bible and synthesizing its message theologically, while also evaluating the other approaches. In the final section of this stimulating book, three additional scholars offer their response to all four views as well as their own take on the subject.

7

What's So Bad about "Textjacking"?

Present yourself to God as one approved, a worker who does not need to be ashamed and who correctly handles the word of truth.

2 Timothy 2:15 TNIV

A reporter and an editor with the *Detroit News* together coined the word "carjacking" in August 1991 to describe the violent effort to steal a Suzuki Sidekick that resulted in its twenty-two-year-old owner's death. In 1992 carjacking was made a federal crime, and by the mid-1990s about 49,000 attempted carjackings were being reported annually. In some cases, the owner of the car is forced to ride along with or even drive the carjackers to a place they determine. As I write this chapter, the death of an eighty-five-year-old woman from southwest Illinois is being reported. Her body was discovered in the trunk of her car after three carjackers abandoned it at their East St. Louis destination.

John Dunham of the International Bible Society recently coined the expression "verse jacking" to describe the misappropriation of biblical texts. Presumably derived from the word "carjacking," this metaphor implies more than simply taking texts to application destinations that the original authors never envisioned. Presumably, Moses would not have anticipated the way Paul applied the law forbidding the muzzling of a grain-treading ox (Deut. 25:4) to the issue of paying Christian ministers fairly (1 Cor. 9:7–12; 1 Tim. 5:18). Rather, the term implies that the interpreters are forcibly using a text for their own selfish—even violent—purposes *against the will* of the text's owner (that is, divine and human authors). Dunham's use of such a strong term suggests that he thinks verse jacking should be taken seriously.[1] I have not tried to keep statistics on how many "attempted textjackings" occur each year. But unlike carjackings they are *always* successful because the original author is unable to put up a fight. As chapters 3–6 illustrate, no biblical text is safe. Misinterpretation pervades Christian publications and can also be found in abundance in weekly sermons, devotional guides, and personal websites.

In writing this book, I have intentionally delayed defending my critique of the common misuse of Scripture until the final chapter. My goal in the preceding six chapters has been to gather "evidence" from a wide range of sources, seeking in each example to demonstrate that a biblical text had been, in most cases, both misinterpreted and misapplied. My intention, however, was also to show how, by giving careful attention to aspects of context, word meaning, genre, and the text's original emphasis and message, we can interpret these texts more accurately and apply them more appropriately.

In this chapter my goal is to make a final plea for taking the divine and human authors' original intentions more seriously when handling Scripture. I will begin by considering and responding to five possible objections to my approach: (1) that I am being judgmental, (2) that I am suggesting that only professional biblical scholars are able to interpret the Bible correctly, (3) that I am denying the role of the Holy Spirit in illuminating interpreters, (4) that I am ignoring the fact that there are—sometimes many—competing interpretations of a given text, and (5) that I am more concerned with correct interpretation than with edifying the church of Jesus Christ. Then I will offer five reasons why we cannot just ignore the problem that I have highlighted in this book before concluding with a positive summary, offering basic tips for preventing "textjacking."

On Judgmentalism and Hermeneutical Nitpicking

So what's so bad about textjacking and other forms of misinterpretation? In his final New Testament letter, the apostle Paul gives young Pastor Tim instructions about how to lead, care for, protect, and strengthen the church in Ephesus. In this passage, Paul challenges Timothy to combat false teaching about the resurrection, which "will spread like gangrene" if left unchecked (2 Tim. 2:17–18), and to avoid "foolish and stupid arguments," which merely "produce quarrels" (v. 23). He also encourages Timothy to model the proper use of God's truthful Word. This is a foundational expectation of all Christian workers: "Do your best to present yourself to God as one approved, a worker who does not need to be ashamed and who correctly handles the word of truth" (2 Tim. 2:15). Old Testament scholar and former seminary president Walter Kaiser Jr. told me and my classmates that he was always careful "to keep his finger on the [biblical] text," seeking to determine its exact meaning, because he "did not wish to hold up the line on Judgment Day." Accordingly, 2 Timothy 2:15 has continually motivated and chastened me to be a more careful interpreter of the Bible. It has also given me a rationale for writing this book. Or am I simply promoting "foolish and stupid arguments" (v. 23)?

Before discussing more fully why I see "textjacking" as such a serious problem, let us examine five reasons someone might give for simply being satisfied with the hermeneutical status quo in the church.

Avoiding Judgmentalism

What is involved in correctly handling Scripture? In a book developing the profile of the "virtuous reader," Richard Briggs emphasizes the importance of humility, wisdom, trust, charity, and receptivity for those who aspire to become skilled interpreters of God's Word.[2] Although Briggs clearly displays interpretive skills in examining a number of Old Testament narratives, he highlights character rather than methods or tools in his book. This reminds me of the sobering warning in 1 Corinthians 13:2 that, even if I "can fathom all mysteries and all knowledge, . . . but do not have love, I am nothing." Writing a book like this can be hazardous to a person's spiritual health. A "gotcha" attitude can replace a love for the Bible, for the truth, for the church, and for influential Christian writers. I vividly recall commenting on the chapel message of a college staff member working in the area of student development who had mentored hundreds of students, preparing them for short-term ministries in the Chicago area and overseas. I simply noted in my biblical interpretation class that his use of the phrase "we have this treasure in jars of clay" in 2 Corinthians 4:7 reflected no knowledge of its historical-cultural background. Weeks later when filling out the course evaluation, one of my students blasted me for criticizing a godly man who was having such a significant spiritual impact on campus.

Does Christian charity preclude critiquing the interpretive work of others? First of all, in pointing out errors in interpretation and application, I am *not* raising doubts about any author's sincerity, intellectual ability, spiritual maturity, or theological orthodoxy. As noted in chapter 2, misinterpretation can have a number of different causes. An interpreter may be unintentionally driven to misinterpretation by a strong desire to defend a specific viewpoint or by a particular set of theological assumptions. We all come to the biblical text with certain presuppositions about what the text says and often with ideas about how we want to use the text for our own purposes. When I point out specific examples of poor interpretation, I am not necessarily suggesting that a cited author's work as a whole is characterized by poor interpretive practice. Many of the biblical texts they cite may be used correctly.

Second, whenever authors publish anything, thereby entering the public marketplace of ideas, they are claiming to have written something worth reading and heeding, and at the same time inviting critical evaluation. The great dialogue of public discourse in which we all engage is an ongoing quest for truth. None of us has a corner on the truth; instead we all continually need to learn from one another. The alternative to critique is a slide into postmodern relativism in which everyone's opinion is equally valid. Under such circumstances, those who shout the loudest are the most likely to be heard! A love for Scripture and the church compels us to undertake measures that may be perceived by some as unloving. Hopefully, such critique will be constructive so that, just as "iron sharpens iron, so one person sharpens another" (Prov. 27:17).

Promoting Professional Scholarship Rather than the Priesthood of All Believers

Followers of Judaism and Christianity have long embraced their designation as "people of the Book."[3] For Christians, especially

Protestants, this is grounded in a twofold conviction: (1) the Bible is divinely inspired and therefore authoritative for the ongoing life of the church and of individual believers, and (2) it is essential that all believers regularly read the Bible and live according to its teachings. The Reformation emphasis on the priesthood of all believers was linked to a conviction that the Scriptures are basically clear and understandable. This led to a renewed effort to translate them from the Latin, read only by a few, into the vernacular languages, read by the masses.

Although I have used the terms "interpreters," "(mis)interpretation," and "hermeneutics" repeatedly in this book, what I am seeking to promote is simply *reading with understanding* and *appropriate application*. In a book like this with discussions of interpretive errors that can get a bit technical—focusing on Hebrew word meaning or the details of Greco-Roman culture—there is a danger of scaring off some readers. And it can wrongly give the impression that you need an advanced degree in biblical studies in order to interpret the Bible correctly. I teach an annual graduate course in biblical interpretation in which most of the students are preparing to be licensed clinical psychologists. They are experts in various stages of human psychological development and are learning to diagnose and treat various mental disorders. But they are sometimes intimidated by the technical aspects of biblical interpretation. "If there are so many ways biblical interpretation can go wrong," they say, "then we might as well leave it up to the experts."

This book was written out of the conviction that, while even experts can misinterpret texts, anyone can—and should—become a better reader of Scripture. Learning to interpret Scripture can be compared with learning a sport. Mastering the fundamental rules and skills of the sport is followed by hours of practice working on more advanced skills. But even professional athletes occasionally need to work on the fundamentals again. Anyone capable of reading this book is capable not only of mastering the basic skills of interpretation but also of evaluating the interpretive claims of others.

I have also sought to point out the rich variety of tools—the fruits of the labors of biblical studies professionals—that are available on the internet, in Christian bookstores, and in good church libraries. Most Bible readers in America could purchase and consult a one-volume commentary or a study Bible when seeking to understand and use a text. Doing so would help direct them toward the proper interpretive path and keep them from straying off into dangerous territory.

Quenching the Holy Spirit

Some of the authors discussed in the preceding chapters claim to have been directed by God in their selection and use of biblical texts. For example, Dr. Bill Hamon begins his foreword to *Breaking the Threefold Demonic Cord* by stating, "God has anointed Sandie Freed with the Spirit of wisdom and revelation. She has the same anointing as the sons of Issachar [see 1 Chron. 12:32], who discerned what God's people should do to gain victory over their enemies."[4] These authors claim a God-given origin and authority for what they have written. This would seem to make their writing exempt from critical evaluation. If they have used Scripture as the Spirit directed them, who am I to criticize—and thereby reject—the work of the Spirit? Could such criticism verge on "blasphemy against the Spirit" (Matt. 12:31)?

I have already discussed the contribution of the Holy Spirit to the interpretive process in some detail in chapter 2, so I will respond only briefly here. Jesus compares the work of the Spirit with the effects of the wind in John 3:8, indicating that, like the wind, we cannot control or necessarily comprehend what the Spirit is doing. But just as an insurance agency can evaluate a claim to determine whether the damage was caused by a violent burst of wind or by something else, so we can examine the claim that a specific spiritual effect is the result of the Spirit's work (1 Cor. 12:3). We can analyze, for example, how the Spirit directed New Testament authors in their interpretive reuse of the Old Testament, assuming that the Spirit would lead contemporary interpreters in a similar direction. Furthermore, it is fair to ask how the earliest interpreters of Scripture most likely understood a particular biblical text since our understanding and application of the text today should be in line with its original meaning as well. Claiming the Spirit's direction as a "trump card" is dangerous to the spiritual health of the church. A balanced perspective is found in Paul's closing instructions to the church in Thessalonica: "Do not quench the Spirit. Do not treat prophecies with contempt but test them all; hold on to what is good, reject every kind of evil" (1 Thess. 5:19–22).

Ignoring the Acknowledged Diversity of Interpreters and Interpretation

It is likely that each of us have found ourselves at some time in a group Bible study where various opinions about the meaning of a biblical text were shared. Sometimes these individual comments are provoked by the question "What does this verse mean to you?" Often the person in charge—today the preferred designation is "discussion leader"—makes no effort to distinguish between interpretive suggestions that are likely or plausible and those that are unlikely or really "off the wall." Instead, each participant is similarly affirmed: "That's a great idea!" or "I never thought of that." Such an approach to biblical study is quite common and can lend support to the conclusion that there is no one *correct* interpretation of a biblical text to be found. Sociologist Christian Smith has recently described the state of contemporary evangelical hermeneutics as resulting in "pervasive interpretive pluralism."[5]

Recent hermeneutical theorists have gone beyond such observed popular pluralism to set forth the implications of postmodernism for biblical interpretation. They speak of the "perspectival" nature of truth, asserting that truth is subjective rather than objective. The foundational role of the reader then is not simply to *discover* meaning but rather to *make* meaning. Generating mutually exclusive interpretations becomes a good thing rather than a problem. Postmodernists emphasize the ambiguity of the biblical text, leading to the conclusion that there is no one correct interpretation. Instead, they either assert that the divine author *intended* multiple meanings or jettison the original human author's intention as irrelevant. Thus, claiming that one interpretation is correct and another incorrect is viewed as an arrogant power grab. Some postmodernists even downplay the importance of the traditional interpretive task. As Old Testament scholar Doug Ingram expresses it, "I do not think we always need to seek for 'the meaning' of a biblical text. . . . Reading the Bible is not always about what it *means* to the reader. Sometimes it is about what it *does* to the reader."[6]

All of this prompts the question of whether I have any warrant for my claim that some interpretations are incorrect. Despite the risk of offering too brief a series of responses to a complex and much debated issue, I would defend my approach on the basis of several considerations. First, even those who argue that a specific biblical text can support more than one meaning or prompt a plurality of viable applications are not promoting interpretive anarchy. To claim that a text means more than one thing is not to claim that it can mean anything. Second, according to Old Testament scholar John Goldingay, some parts of Scripture are characterized by having more than one meaning or being irreducibly ambiguous. In fact, in his opinion, this is true of all biblical texts to some degree.[7] This may overstate the situation. For just as a detective does not need to gather and make sense of every possible clue in a criminal case in order to correctly determine who has committed the crime, so an interpreter does not need to understand every detail of a text in order to correctly interpret the text as a whole. Moreover, at an earlier stage in the investigation, that detective may still be deciding between two suspects but already know enough to eliminate all others. Similarly, an interpreter's uncertainty about what a text *must* mean need not entail an uncertainty about what that text *could* mean or, even less, an uncertainty about what the text *does not* mean. Divine communication becomes ineffective, even impossible, if a given text can mean both "x" and "not x"!

Third, 2 Peter 3:16–17 issues a warning to guard against the repeated distortion of Scripture: "[Paul's] letters contain some things that are hard to understand, which ignorant and unstable people distort, as they do the other Scriptures, to their own destruction. Therefore, dear friends, since you have been forewarned, be on your guard so that you may not be carried away by the error. . . ." And Proverbs 26:9 warns that biblical texts (here, a proverb) can be misused and even dangerous: "Like a thornbush in a drunkard's hand is a proverb in the mouth of a fool." This suggests that there is a correct interpretation and use of specific biblical texts and that the church is charged to be hermeneutically, and not just theologically, vigilant.

Fourth, some would argue that the current "pervasive interpretive pluralism" raises fundamental questions about the Reformation doctrine of the "clarity of Scripture." If the meaning of Scripture is clear, then why are there so many differences of opinion about how we should interpret particular texts and synthesize key doctrines? And if the meaning of Scripture is not clear, then how can we call certain interpretations incorrect? But this doctrine is often misunderstood. According to Goldingay, "To affirm the clarity of scripture is not to claim that it is *immediately clear* to anyone but to affirm that its meaning is in principle *accessible* to anyone and to deny the necessity of arbitrary or high-handed interpretation."[8] Furthermore, this does not mean that all biblical texts are equally clear, but that the Bible taken as a whole expresses with sufficient clarity what followers of Jesus Christ *must* believe and what God-pleasing, holy living involves.

Fifth, some recent hermeneutics publications have distinguished between the "underdetermined" and "overdetermined" nature of the biblical text.[9] Returning to our detective metaphor, some believe that too few clues are available at the crime scene to make a final decision about whom to charge with the crime. Instead, they are content to view various suspects as equally fitting the available clues, in effect giving up on convicting one of them. Others suggest that there are so many clues available at the crime scene that no one detective is capable of gathering and analyzing all of them. A team of detectives working together, however, will do a more complete job of interpreting all of the clues so that nothing crucial is ignored. When each detective, in turn, summarizes the evidence they have gathered, the individual reports may differ without necessarily conflicting.

Similarly, biblical texts are so rich with meaning that various interpreters may offer different perspectives on a given text and bring out different emphases without necessarily offering contradictory interpretations. Therefore, affirming that there may be multiple correct interpretations of a text does not necessarily entail pluralism since each accurate interpretation may reflect only part of the same picture. A text understood within the fuller context of the entire biblical canon will mean *more* than the text viewed solely within its immediate context, but that "greater" meaning will be in continuity with its "lesser" meaning. For example, our understanding of the significance and fulfillment of the Jewish Passover is enriched when John the Baptist says of Jesus, "Look, the Lamb of God, who takes away the sin of the world!" (John 1:29); when Jesus inaugurates the "Lord's Supper" during the time of the annual Passover observance (Matt. 26:19–30); and when Paul announces that "Christ, our Passover lamb, has been sacrificed" (1 Cor. 5:7). But it does not reduce the historical and ceremonial importance of the Jewish holy day.

Subordinating Edification to "Interpretive Correctness"

A final response someone might make to my emphasis on correct interpretation would be to argue that, in the process, I may be losing sight of the primary purpose of Scripture (and its interpretation)—edification. Briggs points to Augustine (AD 354–430), for whom "the goal and framing context for all Christian interpretation is the love of God and the love of neighbor,"[10] based on Matthew 22:35–40. Augustine sets forth this principle in his classic work, *On Christian Teaching*:

> So anyone who thinks that he has understood the divine scriptures or any part of them, but cannot by his understanding build up this double

love of God and neighbor, has not yet succeeded in understanding them. Anyone who derives from them an idea which is useful for supporting this love but fails to say what the writer demonstrably meant in the passage has not made a fatal error, and is certainly not a liar.[11]

Briggs summarizes Augustine's point here as follows: "in the short term, love trumps exegesis."[12]

Someone could understand Augustine as affirming that "the end justifies the means." In other words, as long as our interpretation of Scripture edifies the church (by fostering the twofold love of God and neighbor), it really does not matter how accurately we interpret it (that is, whether our interpretation is in keeping with the original author's intention). But to suggest this would be to miss Augustine's larger point in this quote, in this paragraph, and in the book. In the quoted sentence, the crucial word is "*fatal* error." Though well-intentioned, it is nevertheless an error, and Augustine's primary aim here is to correct it. So he goes on to say:

> If . . . he is misled by an idea of the kind that builds up love, . . . he is misled in the same way as a walker who leaves his path by mistake but reaches the destination to which the path leads by going through a field. But he must be put right and shown how it is more useful not to leave the path, in case the habit of deviating should force him to go astray or even adrift.[13]

Accordingly, edification-driven misinterpreters of Scripture should not be condemned but also not be affirmed in their interpretive practices.

To summarize this section, none of the basic objections to my critique is compelling. Pointing out an author's interpretive errors does not constitute an attack on that author's character; in fact, our understanding of Scripture advances through the balanced evaluation of the interpretive work of others. The Reformation emphasis on the priesthood of believers also entails a call for all believers to learn to handle God's Word properly, so claiming the Holy Spirit's guidance in coming up with a questionable interpretation is a dangerous practice for the church to accept. The fact that varying interpretations of a given text have been proposed does not mean that no correct interpretation exists or that all interpretative suggestions are equally valid. Finally, edifying but flawed interpretations are not to be affirmed, since that simply reinforces an improper approach to Scripture.

Augustine's larger purpose in *On Christian Teaching* is stated near the conclusion of his preface: "the teacher who teaches how to under-stand scripture is like the teacher of the alphabet, one who teaches how to read."[14] And he focuses in book three on setting forth and il-lustrating rules for correctly interpreting difficult types of texts: figura-tive expressions, commands and prohibitions, obscure or ambiguous passages, and texts that appear to commend unethical behavior by God or prominent biblical figures. The purpose of the present book, similar to the one Augustine wrote at the end of the fourth century, is to correct the common misuse of the Bible by presenting the ABCs of proper biblical interpretation.

Taking Preventative Measures against "Textjacking"

In concluding this primer, how should we view the many examples we have discussed, as well as the hundreds of additional examples we could have examined? First of all, I agree with Augustine's assessment of the type of interpretive error we are considering in this book: it is not "fatal" and it is definitely not a "sin" (as Augustine puts it, such an interpreter is "not a liar"). I do not have the impression that any of the authors cited intentionally misinterpreted texts for underhanded purposes. But it does appear to me that some of them are careless or untrained interpreters. Their misuse of Scripture is better viewed as a bad hermeneutical habit that should be stopped before it gets worse.

Second, these examples demonstrate how Christians instinctively turn to the Bible to determine and defend their practices, programs, and preferences. Their desire to be "people of the Book" is com-mendable. Yet this does not validate the specific uses that they often make of the Bible in the process. Their use of individual biblical texts often seems to stem more from an unconscious compulsion to ground their views in Scripture than from any theological necessity. As Christians, we do not need to demonstrate that our practices, programs, and preferences are *biblical* in order for them to be valid and useful, as long as they are not clearly *unbiblical*. It is better to allow them to remain *abiblical* (that is, not addressed by Scripture) than to heavy-handedly force some text to somehow support them. We must be content to acknowledge that the Bible as an ancient book is simply not interested in many of the issues that are the hot topics in society and the church today. When we affirm the sufficiency of Scripture, we are merely acknowledging that Scripture is a sufficient basis for Christian faith and practice, not that we can expect to find an apt verse for every occasion or foible.

Third, these interpreters are usually not falling into heresy or unbiblical practices in the process of misinterpreting specific texts. More often than not it is simply a matter of deriving the *right* doctrines or ethical principles from the *wrong* texts.[15] It is important to note, however, that James Sire identifies some of the same "techniques" that we have discussed in this book as he analyzes the various ways in which the cults "misread the Bible." These include ignoring the immediate context, collapsing contexts (treating two or more unrelated texts as if they belonged together), and mistaking figurative language for literal and vice versa.[16] And in some cases, we have identified rather questionable claims that are presented as correct largely on the basis of the cited biblical texts.

Fourth, by incorrectly grounding their claims in biblical texts, these authors are basically usurping biblical authority to support their own ideas. Proposals that might otherwise be more easily dismissed by the reader may be accepted because they are apparently backed by Scripture. When biblical authority is invoked in connection with an obviously misinterpreted or misapplied passage, the authority of none other than the divine author is potentially being abused. In introducing a lengthy study of how Scripture is used in broader social-ethical debates, Manfred Brauch freely speaks of "abusing Scripture" when an author is involved in "interpreting and applying the Bible in questionable or irresponsible ways." He explains that he "very deliberately chose the term *abuse* to point to the serious nature of misreading the Bible." Inevitably, "violence is done to its message and meaning."[17]

Finally, at best, this habit of misinterpretation promotes a faulty view of how God speaks to the church today through his Word. Psychologist Dan Allender describes Christians "who have found comfort in Bible passages when the meaning has been twisted beyond comprehension" or when these passages "have been forced to bear a perspective that was simply not to be found in the verse, yet they were encouraged or convicted as a result of their understanding."[18] These individuals are too easily satisfied with this kind of minimal spiritual diet rather than enjoying the succulent delights of meaty scriptural texts that require some "chewing." As Hebrews 5:13–14 states, "Anyone who lives on milk, being still an infant, is not acquainted with the teaching about righteousness. But solid food is for the mature, who by constant use have trained themselves to distinguish good from evil." Why be satisfied with junk food just because it fills the stomach?

Some of the authors I have cited in this book might defend their practice by protesting, "But I wasn't actually *interpreting* those texts—I was simply *using* them!" This attitude implies that there is no necessary connection between a text's original meaning and its appropriate application today. At worst, such an approach could give the impression that the Bible can say anything we want or need it to say. The role that the Bible has played in the cultural debates over slavery, war, and gay marriage should warn us against treating this habit as innocuous.[19] Pastoral counselor Jay Adams states the matter bluntly: "To use the Bible in a shallow, simplistic fashion that in many cases misrepresents what God is saying in the passage . . . is inexcusable."[20] Too high a percentage of today's bestselling Christian books consistently model an approach to biblical interpretation that their readers should not seek to imitate!

We should not expect God to speak effectively to the church today through snippets of decontextualized Bible verses that are strung together like beads on a necklace. Nor should we assume that he prefers to speak through isolated Bible mottos, however strikingly formulated they may be. God has given us his Word in a richly diverse canonical collection. He spoke to his people throughout the centuries of biblical history in specific times and circumstances and then preserved that record within the community of faith. And it is through this biblical record that he continues to speak to us today. While not requiring us all to become professional biblical scholars, the nature of Scripture prescribes some specific interpretive steps if it is our desire to be someone "who correctly handles the word of truth" (2 Tim. 2:15):

1. **Care about understanding:** We must be willing to devote sufficient time to studying each text so that we may understand it on its own terms *before* using it in contemporary applications.
2. **Catch nuance:** We should acknowledge that our use of even familiar verses whose meaning seems to be completely clear can be enriched and made more precise by looking at them more closely.
3. **Clarify context:** We should avoid using any verse or half verse without examining how the verses that immediately precede and follow it help us determine its exact meaning and function.
4. **Check terms:** If our use of a biblical text emphasizes a specific word or words, it is advisable to look that word up in a concordance or theological dictionary to get a clearer idea of its range of uses in the Bible.

5. **Consider genre:** We should reflect on how the particular genre of the text we are studying (such as narrative, proverb, letter, prophetic oracle, or law) affects both how divine truth is communicated through it and how it can be applied appropriately.
6. **Consult experts:** We should consult appropriate resources—such as Bible dictionaries, background reference works, and commentaries—to help solve interpretive problems and avoid interpretive errors. A good study Bible is always a valuable friend of the interpreter.
7. **Correlate application:** After deciding on the contemporary use or application we would like to make of a text, we should reflect on how closely it is related to the text's original meaning. We should also think about how the first readers of the text might have responded to it and how similar our situation today is to theirs.

Think about It

1. Which of the five reasons (discussed above) for being satisfied with the hermeneutical status quo in the church do you find the most persuasive? Why?
2. As you read during the coming week, keep on the lookout for biblical quotations and allusions. When you find a biblical reference, take the time to look it up and ask yourself whether the modern author seems to be using it appropriately.
3. A recent "letter to the editor" in our local newspaper begins by quoting part of Luke 12:48: "From everyone who has been given much, much will be demanded." The writer uses this verse as the basis for recommending that the tax rate for the wealthiest Americans should be increased. Why do you think he cited a Bible verse in discussing income tax policy? Do you think he is using this verse appropriately? Why or why not?

Read about It

1. After reading numerous examples of misused biblical texts, it should be refreshing to read something written by authors who use the Bible well. The coauthored books by psychologist

Dan Allender and Old Testament scholar Tremper Longman III offer powerful examples of how the careful analysis of complete chapters and even entire books can provide a secure biblical basis for life-changing counsel. *Bold Love* (Colorado Springs: NavPress, 1992) draws on Longman's biblical-theological study of the image of God as a divine warrior; *The Cry of the Soul* (Colorado Springs: NavPress, 1994) focuses on select psalms; *Intimate Allies* (Wheaton, IL: Tyndale, 1995) draws on a wide range of texts, including Song of Songs and Proverbs 31; *The Intimate Mystery* (Downers Grove, IL: InterVarsity, 2005) expounds on Genesis 2:24–25; and *Breaking the Idols of Your Heart* (Downers Grove, IL: InterVarsity, 2007) works through the entire book of Ecclesiastes.

2. Although describing some key interpretive steps, I have not tried to offer a full guide to interpreting biblical texts. If reading this book has whetted your appetite for more, consider reading one of the following books: David R. Bauer and Robert A. Traina, *Inductive Bible Study: A Comprehensive Guide to the Practice of Hermeneutics* (Grand Rapids: Baker, 2011); Jeannine K. Brown, *Scripture as Communication: Introducing Biblical Hermeneutics* (Grand Rapids: Baker Academic, 2007); Robert H. Stein, *A Basic Guide to Interpreting the Bible: Playing by the Rules*, 2nd ed. (Grand Rapids: Baker, 2011); T. Norton Sterrett and Richard L. Schultz, *How to Understand Your Bible*, 3rd ed. (Downers Grove, IL: InterVarsity, 2010); Mark L. Strauss, *How to Read the Bible in Changing Times: Understanding and Applying God's Word Today* (Grand Rapids: Baker, 2011).

Notes

Introduction

1. I will offer a fuller explanation regarding why this is problematic in chapter 7.

2. Richard Schultz, "Praying Jabez's Prayer: Turning an Obscure Biblical Narrative into a Miracle-Working Mantra," *Trinity Journal* 24 (2003): 113–19.

3. Richard Schultz, "Responsible Hermeneutics for Wisdom Literature," in *Care for the Soul: Exploring the Intersection of Psychology and Theology*, ed. M. R. McMinn and T. R. Phillips (Downers Grove, IL: InterVarsity, 2001), 254–75. This was published in an earlier form as "Im Wort gegründet? Ein Ruf zum verantwortlichen Umgang mit der Bibel in der christlichen Psychologie," in *Bibel und Gemeinde* 1/98 (1998): 11–20.

4. Richard Schultz, "'For I Did Not Shrink from Declaring to You the Whole Purpose of God': Biblical Theology's Role within Christian Counseling," in *Edification: The Transdisciplinary Journal of Christian Psychology* 4 (2010): 47–55.

Chapter 1 The "Jabez Prayer" Phenomenon

1. Bruce Wilkinson, *The Prayer of Jabez: Breaking through to the Blessed Life* (Sisters, OR: Multnomah, 2000).

2. Kenneth Woodward, "Platitudes or Prophecy?," *Newsweek*, August 27, 2001, 47.

3. This summary is gleaned from Wilkinson's own explanations on pages 18–75.

4. Jabez's name (Hebrew *ya'bets*) is formed by reversing the second and third consonants in the Hebrew word for "pain" (*'otseb*).

5. "Jabez Testimonies," anonymous comment, Prayer of Jabez website, January 23, 2001, http://www.prayerofjabez.com, accessed April 25, 2002.

6. "Unanswered Prayers: In Swaziland, U.S. Preacher Sees His Dream Vanish," *Wall Street Journal*, December 19, 2005, http://online.wsj.com/article/SB113495910699726095-email.html, accessed May 5, 2008.

7. Bruce Wilkinson, *Beyond Jabez: Expanding Your Borders* (Sisters, OR: Multnomah, 2005), 13.

8. Richard Bauckham, *Jude, 2 Peter*, Word Biblical Commentary 50 (Waco: Word, 1983), 331.

9. Ibid., 335.

Chapter 2 The Roots of Faulty Interpretation

1. Donald Lee Petry, *I Have Found an Elephant in the Bible* (Cedar Grove, IN: self-published, 1974), 1.

2. David Barton, cited in Jacques Berlinerblau, *Thumpin' It: The Use and Abuse of the Bible in Today's Presidential Politics* (Louisville: Westminster John Knox, 2008), 27.

3. See the helpful discussion by Vern S. Poythress, "What Does God Say through Human Authors?," in Harvie M. Conn, ed., *Inerrancy and Hermeneutic: A Tradition, A Challenge, A Debate* (Grand Rapids: Baker, 1988), 81–99.

4. I will discuss the nature and use of Bible translations and basic principles for determining word meaning more fully in chapter 4.

5. This is reflected on the cover of a recent book by Old Testament scholar Kenton L. Sparks, *God's Word in Human Words* (Grand Rapids: Baker, 2008), which uses differing font sizes to emphasize *Human Words* in the title. An overemphasis on either feature of the Bible can tend to skew our understanding of the nature of Scripture.

6. See, for example, Grant R. Jeffrey, *The Signature of God—Astonishing Biblical Discoveries* (Nashville: Word, 1998), esp. chaps. 10–12: "The Mysterious Hebrew Codes," "The Name of Jesus Encoded in the Old Testament," and "The Mathematical Signature of God in the Words of Scripture."

7. Jeffrey Satinover, *Cracking the Bible Code* (New York: William Morrow, 1997), 161–82.

8. Scot McKnight, *The Blue Parakeet: Rethinking How You Read the Bible* (Grand Rapids: Zondervan, 2010), 46–47. McKnight remarks, with tongue in cheek, however, that no one has made a similar collection of biblical warnings, creating a "Wrath of God Calendar of Warnings" (47). Not all of the biblical texts that Alice Chapin includes in her *365 Bible Promises for Busy People* (Wheaton, IL: Tyndale House, 1992) actually contain a promise. For example, #347 consists solely of commands taken from Eph. 5:33 and 6:1, 4: "Let each one of you . . . so love his own wife as himself, and let the wife see that she respects her husband. Children, obey your parents in the Lord.

... Fathers, do not provoke your children to wrath, but bring them up in the training and admonition of the Lord" (NKJV). Ironically, she has omitted Eph. 6:2–3, which contains a striking promise (195).

9. Gerhard Hasel, *Old Testament Theology: Basic Issues in the Current Debate*, 4th ed. (Grand Rapids: Eerdmans, 1991), 204.

10. William W. Klein, Craig L. Blomberg, and Robert L. Hubbard, *Introduction to Biblical Interpretation*, rev. ed. (Nashville: Thomas Nelson, 2004), 4.

11. Millard J. Erickson, *Evangelical Interpretation: Perspectives on Hermeneutical Issues* (Grand Rapids: Baker, 1993), 52.

12. Ibid., 54.

13. Peter Enns, *Inspiration and Incarnation: Evangelicals and the Problem of the Old Testament* (Grand Rapids: Baker, 2005), 114–16. The italics in the quotations are his.

14. See, for example, the critical exchanges between Enns, Darrell L. Bock, and Walter C. Kaiser Jr., in *Three Views on the New Testament Use of the Old Testament*, ed. Kenneth Berding and Jonathan Lunde (Grand Rapids: Zondervan, 2008).

15. Philo of Alexandria, *On the Special Laws* 4.106–7 (*The Contemplative Life, the Giants, and Selections*, trans. David Winston [New York: Paulist Press, 1981], 283).

16. Origen, *Homily on Luke* 34.3 (*Origen: Homilies on Luke*, trans. Joseph T. Lienhard, Fathers of the Church 94 [Washington, DC: Catholic University of America Press, 1996], 138).

17. Martin Luther, *Lectures on Genesis, Chapters 26–30*, ed. J. J. Pelikan and W. A. Hansen, trans. G. V. Schick and P. D. Pahl, Luther's Works 5 (St. Louis: Concordia, 1968), 347.

18. David C. Steinmetz, "The Superiority of Pre-Critical Exegesis," in *The Theological Interpretation of Scripture: Classic and Contemporary Readings*, ed. Stephen E. Fowl (Oxford: Blackwell, 1997), 29.

19. For a helpful discussion of what we can learn from the early Christian interpretation of Scripture, see Daniel J. Treier, *Introducing Theological Interpretation of Scripture: Recovering a Christian Practice* (Grand Rapids: Baker Academic, 2008), esp. chap. 1: "Recovering the Past: Imitating Precritical Interpretation," 39–55.

Chapter 3 The Consequences of Ignoring Context

1. The origin of this saying is unclear. New Testament scholar D. A. Carson attributes the saying to his pastor father ("One Way [Matthew 7:13–27]," in *Only One Way? Reaffirming the Exclusive Truth Claims of Christianity*, ed. Richard D. Phillips [Wheaton, IL: Crossway, 2007], 133–34).

2. For example, John H. Hayes and Frederick C. Prussner, *Old Testament Theology: Its History and Development* (Atlanta: John Knox, 1985), 15–19, refer to "proof text" theologies in the sixteenth and seventeenth centuries.

3. Henry Cloud and John S. Townsend, *Boundaries: When to Say Yes, When to Say No to Take Control of Your Life* (Grand Rapids: Zondervan, 1992), 233.

4. John Eldredge, *Wild at Heart: Discovering the Secret of a Man's Soul* (Nashville: Thomas Nelson, 2001), 187.

5. Anne Ortlund, *Disciplines of the Beautiful Woman* (Waco: Word, 1977), 97.

6. John Crowder, *Miracle Workers, Reformers, and the New Mystics* (Shippensburg, PA: Destiny Image, 2006), 25.

7. The NIV clearly indicates that Paul's reference may be more limited by translating "I can do all this. . . ," requiring the reader, in turn, to examine the context to determine what he means by "this."

8. For example, according to Leon Morris, *Gospel According to Matthew* (Grand Rapids: Eerdmans, 1992), 469–71, a "little section on prayer" begins in Matthew 18:19, the initial word "again" signaling "a fresh start" and "two or three" referring to "the smallest possible group." D. A. Carson, "Matthew," in *The Expositor's Bible Commentary*, ed. Tremper Longman III and David E. Garland, rev. ed. (Grand Rapids: Zondervan, 2010), 9:457, however, restricts the promise "about anything" in verse 19 to "about any judicial matter" and understands "two or three" as referring to "judges solemnly convened before the church."

9. Dan Montgomery, *Finding Your Way: A Christian Guide to Transforming Your Personality and Relationships* (Minneapolis: Augsburg, 1999), 76–77.

10. Lawrence J. Crabb Jr., *The Marriage Builder* (Grand Rapids: Zondervan, 1982), 68.

11. Ibid., 69.

12. John Eldredge and Stasi Eldredge, *Captivating: Unveiling the Mystery of a Woman's Soul* (Nashville: Nelson, 2005), 156–58.

13. See, for example, Teresa J. Hornsby, *Sex Texts from the Bible: Selections Annotated & Explained* (Woodstock, VT: SkyLight Paths, 2007), 4, 8; but see also the detailed refutation of this viewpoint by Daniel I. Block, *Judges, Ruth*, New American Commentary 6 (Nashville: Broadman & Holman, 1999), 683–96.

14. Eldredge and Eldredge, *Captivating*, 157.

15. James C. Dobson and Shirley Dobson, *Night Light: A Devotional for Couples* (Sisters, OR: Multnomah, 2000), 135–36.

16. William W. Klein, Craig L. Blomberg, and Robert L. Hubbard, *Introduction to Biblical Interpretation*, 2nd ed. (Dallas: Word, 2004), 239.

17. Rob Bell, *Velvet Elvis: Repainting the Christian Faith* (Grand Rapids: Zondervan, 2005), 133–34.

18. Craig G. Bartholomew and Michael W. Goheen, *The Drama of Scripture: Finding Our Place in the Biblical Story* (Grand Rapids: Baker, 2004), 27, distinguish six acts and an interlude: God Establishes His Kingdom: Creation; Rebellion in the Kingdom: Fall; The King Chooses Israel: Redemption Initiated; Interlude: A Kingdom Story Waiting for an Ending: The Intertestamental Period; The Coming of the King: Redemption Accomplished; Spreading the News of the King: The Mission of the Church; The Return of the King: Redemption Completed.

19. Jay E. Adams, *From Forgiven to Forgiving* (Wheaton: Victor, 1989), 151–53.

20. Because Psalm 51 is a favorite psalm of repentance, verse 11 is frequently referred to in popular Christian books. Most authors citing this verse recognize the problem with praying this as a Christian, as noted above. For example, Stormie Omartian, in *The Power of a Praying Life: Finding the Freedom, Wholeness, and True Success God Has for You* (Eugene, OR: Harvest House, 2010), 84, writes, "Because Jesus has come and given the Holy Spirit to those who receive Him, the Spirit doesn't leave us unless we deliberately reject Him." Other authors avoid mentioning the Holy Spirit here, referring merely to God's "presence," or cite verse 11 as the prayer of David without raising the question of whether we should pray the same words today.

21. Frank B. Minirth and Paul D. Meier, *Happiness Is a Choice: A Manual on the Symptoms, Causes, and Cures of Depression* (Grand Rapids: Baker, 1978), 97.

22. Bernard K. Bangley, *Getting Along When You Feel Like Getting Even* (Wheaton: Harold Shaw, 1993), 75.

23. It is true that the Mosaic law contains some instructions that pertain to how the Israelites were to treat animals as well as their agricultural land. The reference to God's "decrees" and "commands" in Leviticus 26:3, however, cannot be limited to such stewardship laws, nor do the Sabbath laws relate exclusively to caring for natural resources.

24. Tommy Tenney, *The God Catchers: Experiencing the Manifest Presence of God* (Nashville: Nelson, 2001).

25. Ibid., 15–17, italics in original.

26. Richard A. Young, *Is God a Vegetarian? Christianity, Vegetarianism, and Animal Rights* (Chicago: Open Court, 1999), 69–71.

27. Ibid., 70.

28. Ibid.

Chapter 4 Divine Truth Expressed in Human Words

1. Lewis Carroll, *Through the Looking-Glass and What Alice Found There* (London: Macmillan, 1872), 124.

2. J. C. Laansma, "2 Timothy, Titus," in *1 & 2 Timothy, Titus, Hebrews*, Cornerstone Biblical Commentary 17 (Carol Stream, IL: Tyndale, 2009), 170.

3. Minirth and Meier, *Happiness Is a Choice*, 98. John F. MacArthur Jr., "The Psychology Epidemic and Its Cure," *Master's Seminary Journal* 2 (1991): 19–20, contrasts professional psychologists with the "quintessential Counselor," Jesus Christ, citing Isaiah 9:6 as support; see also George Scipione, "The Wonderful Counselor, the Other Counselor, and Christian Counseling," *Westminster Theological Journal* 36 (1974): 174–75, who calls Jesus "the greatest psychologist and clinician that has ever lived," similarly referring to Isaiah 9:6.

4. D. A. Carson, *Exegetical Fallacies*, 2nd ed. (Grand Rapids: Baker, 1996), chap. 1.

5. Shirley Cook, *The Exodus Diet Plan* (Old Tappan, NJ: Revell, 1986), 118–19.

6. However, a rabbinic tradition recorded in the Babylonian Talmud tractate Berakhot 17a draws an intriguing parallel: "Now that I have conducted a fast my blood and fat have been reduced. May it truly be thy will that the blood and fat I have lost will be considered as if I offered them up to you upon the altar and you will accept me." Cited by Jacob Milgrom, *Leviticus 1–16*, Anchor Bible 3 (New York: Doubleday, 1991), 214.

7. Rob Reynolds, "Onward Christian Voters: What Is the Biblical Approach to Politics?," *Moody* (September–October 1996): 24–25. For information on the Christian Action Network, see http://www.christianaction.org/ (accessed July 20, 2011). Erwin Lutzer makes a more appropriate use of the parable in "Stewardship Trusting," *Decision* (May 1997): 12–13, although he fails to explain what Matthew 25 means by the word "talents."

8. Jentezen Franklin, *Believe That You Can: Moving with Tenacity toward the Dream God Has Given You* (Lake Mary, FL: Charisma House, 2008), 10–12.

9. The claim of M. Agnes, ed., *Webster's New World College Dictionary*, 4th ed. (Cleveland: Wiley, 2002), xvi, is more modest: "A better understanding of the current usage of a word can often come from a fuller knowledge of the word's history."

10. Robert Hicks, *The Masculine Journey: Understanding the Six Stages of Manhood* (Colorado Springs: NavPress, 1993); see also *The Seasons of a Man's Life* by Daniel J. Levinson (New York: Knopf, 1978), on whose secular research Hicks draws. A second book by Hicks, *In Search of Wisdom* (Colorado Springs: NavPress, 1995), displays the same questionable dependence on alleged etymologies in determining meaning.

11. Hicks, *The Masculine Journey*, 19.

12. James Barr, *The Semantics of Biblical Language* (Oxford: Oxford University Press, 1961), 159.

13. Peter Cotterell and Max Turner, *Linguistics & Biblical Interpretation* (Downers Grove, IL: InterVarsity, 1989), 133. Their prime example is the Greek word *hyperetes*, translated as "servants" in the NIV in 1 Corinthians 4:1. This word is popularly interpreted as deriving from *hypo* = "under" +

eretes = "rower," signifying a rower from the lowest level in a Roman galley, although "there is no hard evidence that the word *ever* meant any such thing, and by the time of the New Testament the word is in wide usage for all types of servants," including some who were "relatively high-ranking." Preachers have commonly used this etymology to commend a "lowly attitude" to Christian ministers.

14. See "II. *'nsh*," in William Gesenius, *A Hebrew and English Lexicon of the Old Testament*, ed. F. Brown, S. R. Driver, and C. A. Briggs, trans. E. Robinson (Oxford: Clarendon, 1972), 60.

15. Hicks, *Masculine Journey*, 188–89.

16. Anne Ortlund, *Children Are Wet Cement* (1995; repr., Lincoln, NE: iUniverse, 2002), 64–65.

17. *Webster's New World College Dictionary*, 4th ed., s.v. "enthusiasm."

18. Creflo A. Dollar Jr., *Total Life Prosperity: 14 Practical Steps to Receiving God's Full Blessing* (Nashville: Nelson, 1999), 46.

19. For example, several commentators suggest that by referring to "water and blood" in 1 John 5:6, 8, John is seeking to evoke (1) the baptism and crucifixion of Jesus, (2) the mixture that flowed out of Jesus's side when speared by a soldier (John 19:34), and (3) the Christian sacraments of baptism and communion, although this seems unlikely.

20. This category label is from Carson, *Exegetical Fallacies*, 4.

21. Robert Schuller, *The Be-Happy Attitudes: Eight Positive Attitudes That Can Transform Your Life!* (Nashville: Nelson, 1997), 76. Schuller's definition is apparently more influenced by his desire to produce the acrostic MEEK (M—mighty; E—emotionally stable; E—educable; K—kind) than by the actual use of this word in the Greek New Testament.

22. See Hornsby, *Sex Texts from the Bible*, 66–71.

23. Gary David Comstock, *Gay Theology without Apology* (Cleveland: Pilgrim, 1993), 87–88.

24. So-called Daniel fasts are newly fashionable in the church today. See Elmer E. Towns, *The Daniel Fast for Spiritual Breakthrough* (Ventura, CA: Regal, 2010), and Grace Bass and Lynda Anderson, *The Daniel's Fast Cookbook* (Brooklyn, NY: A&B, 2008). Daniel 1 appears to describe an exceptional circumstance rather than Daniel's usual preferred diet (see Dan. 10:3).

25. Francis Hunter, *God's Answer to Fat . . . Lose It!* (Houston: Hunter Ministries, 1976), 47.

26. Robert Young, *Analytical Concordance to the Bible* (Grand Rapids: Eerdmans, 1975), 331.

27. Hunter, *God's Answer to Fat*, 47.

28. Michelle McKinney Hammond, *How to Be Blessed and Highly Favored: Flourishing Under the Smile of God* (Colorado Springs: WaterBrook, 2001), 5–6.

29. Ibid., 6.

30. Eugene Carpenter and Michael Grisanti, "'*awen*," in *New International Dictionary of Old Testament Theology & Exegesis*, ed. W. A. VanGemeren (Grand Rapids: Zondervan, 1997), 1:311–12.

31. Bill Hybels and Mark Mittelberg, *Becoming a Contagious Christian* (Grand Rapids: Zondervan, 1994), 45.

32. Ibid.

33. Thomas Champness, *The Young Preacher's Guide to Success*, rev. ed. (1901; repr., Nicholasville, KY: Schmul, 1993), 25.

34. R. Thomas Ashbrook, *Mansions of the Heart: Exploring the Seven Stages of Spiritual Growth* (San Francisco: Jossey-Bass, 2009), 47. The direct source for his mansion metaphor, however, is Saint Teresa of Avila, *The Interior Castle*, Classics of Western Spirituality (New York: Paulist, 1979).

35. *Webster's New World College Dictionary*, 4th ed., s.v. "mansion."

Chapter 5 Understanding the Literary Menu

1. John Goldingay, *Theological Diversity and the Authority of the Old Testament* (Grand Rapids: Eerdmans, 1987), 15, citing Stuart Y. Blanch, *The World Our Orphanage: Studies in the Theology of the Bible* (London: Epworth, 1972), 16.

2. Kevin J. Vanhoozer, "Lost in Interpretation? Truth, Scripture, and Hermeneutics," *Journal of the Evangelical Theological Society* 48 (2005): 104.

3. J. Matthew Sleeth, *Serve God, Save the Planet: A Christian Call to Action* (White River Junction, VT: Chelsea Green, 2006), 59–60.

4. Joshua Harris, *Boy Meets Girl: Say Hello to Courtship* (Sisters, OR: Multnomah, 2000), 53–54.

5. John Eldredge, *The Way of the Wild Heart: A Map of the Masculine Journey* (Nashville: Nelson, 2006), 259.

6. Rick Warren, *The Purpose Driven Life: What On Earth Am I Here For?* (Grand Rapids: Zondervan, 2002), 22–24. The CEV is cited here because that is the Bible version that Warren quotes.

7. Ibid., 25.

8. Bill Sanders, *Seize the Moment, Not Your Teen* (Wheaton: Tyndale House, 1997), 39. This verse is also foundational for Warren's development of *The Purpose Driven Life*, 31.

9. Jack E. Shaw, *Little by Little: A Journey* (Bloomington, IL: CrossBooks, 2009), 136–37.

10. Gary Smalley and John Trent, *The Blessing* (Nashville: Nelson, 1986), 22–24.

11. Gordon D. Fee and Douglas Stuart, *How to Read the Bible for All Its Worth*, 3rd ed. (Grand Rapids: Zondervan, 2003), 92.

12. Eugene H. Peterson, *Growing Up in Christ: A Guide for Families with Adolescents* (Atlanta: John Knox, 1976), 20–23.

13. By "story" I am referring to its use of an unfolding plotline and developing characters; I am not implying that the text is fiction.

14. John C. Maxwell, *Be All You Can Be! A Challenge to Stretch Your God-Given Potential* (Colorado Springs: Cook, 2007), 85.

15. Ibid., 69, 86.

16. But see the description of other oversized Philistine foes in 2 Samuel 21:15–22 and 1 Chronicles 20:4–8.

17. See especially the various viewpoints set forth in Gary T. Meadors, ed., *Four Views on Moving Beyond the Bible to Theology* (Grand Rapids: Zondervan, 2009). Here I am highlighting the views of Walter C. Kaiser Jr., Kevin J. Vanhoozer, and Mark L. Strauss.

18. S. J. Hill, *Burning Desire: The Story of God's Jealous Love for You* (Orlando: Relevant Books, 2005), 14.

19. Ibid., 14–17.

20. See John H. Stek, "Biblical Typology, Yesterday and Today," *Calvin Theological Journal* 5 (1970): 162.

21. John H. Walton and Kim E. Walton, *The Bible Story Handbook: A Resource for Teaching 175 Stories from the Bible* (Wheaton: Crossway, 2010), 66–68.

22. Ibid., 24–25. The parenthetical comments are my summary of the Waltons' lengthier explanation of the fallacy, using their own words as much as possible.

23. Stephen H. Webb, *Good Eating: The Christian Practice of Everyday Life* (Grand Rapids: Brazos, 2001), 76.

24. Michael D. Jacobson, *The Word on Health: A Biblical and Medical Overview of How to Care for Your Body and Mind* (Chicago: Moody, 2000), 125–27.

25. Jacobson seeks to defend his viewpoint by citing the case of Eli and his sons, the priestly family who ate fat and were judged by God as a result (1 Sam. 2:12–17, 29). This text suggests rather that their actual sin was despising God and his prescribed sacrifices and depriving him of what was his due (vv. 29–30).

26. Gordon J. Wenham, *The Book of Leviticus*, New International Commentary on the Old Testament (Grand Rapids: Eerdmans, 1979), 125.

27. Eloise T. Choice, *The Secular and the Sacred Harmonized* (Bloomington, IN: AuthorHouse, 2006), 245.

28. Betty Miller, *Exposing Satan's Devices Workbook* (Dewey, AZ: Christ Unlimited, 1993–2004), 67.

29. Cloud and Townsend, *Boundaries*, 41.

30. Ted A. Hildebrandt, "Proverb," in *Cracking Old Testament Codes: A Guide to Interpreting the Literary Genres of the Old Testament*, ed. D. Brent Sandy and Ronald L. Giese Jr. (Nashville: Broadman & Holman, 1995), 234–37.

31. George M. Schwab Sr., "The Proverbs and the Art of Persuasion," *Journal of Biblical Counseling* 14 (1995): 17.

32. Traditionally "Train up" (ESV, NASB, NKJV).

33. Paul D. Meier cites it seven times in his book *Christian Child-Rearing and Personality Development* (Grand Rapids: Baker, 1977), 18, 45, 92, 123, 151, 159, 160.

34. Cloud and Townsend, *Boundaries*, 62–63.

35. Smalley and Trent, *The Blessing*, 103.

36. Robert Hicks, *In Search of Wisdom: Timeless Insights for the Practice of Life* (Colorado Springs: NavPress, 1995), 120–22.

37. See Ted Hildebrandt, "Proverbs 22:6a: Train Up a Child?," *Grace Theological Journal* 9 (1988): 4–5.

38. Ibid., 3–19.

39. James Allen, *As a Man Thinketh*, rev. ed. (Nashville: Nelson, 2009); Carmen Miranda Thomas, *As a Man Thinketh in His Heart So Is He* (West Conshohocken, PA: Infinity, 2006). Robert S. McGee's book on building self-worth, which has sold more than a million copies, is also grounded in Proverbs 23:7. In *The Search for Significance: Seeing Your True Worth through God's Eyes* (Nashville: Word, 1998), McGee promotes behavior modification by changing "our beliefs about who we are," since our behavior "is usually consistent with what we think to be true about ourselves" (23).

40. See also Tremper Longman III, *Proverbs* (Grand Rapids: Baker, 2006), 425. Longman compares their food with a hair in the throat.

41. Fee and Stuart, *How to Read the Bible for All Its Worth*, 58–59.

42. Robert Lewis, *Raising a Modern-Day Knight: A Father's Role in Guiding His Son to Authentic Manhood* (Colorado Springs: Focus on the Family, 1997), 57–58. Lewis's Scripture citations are from the NASB.

43. Ibid., 59.

44. Joel Osteen, *Your Best Life Now: 7 Steps to Living at Your Full Potential* (New York: Warner Faith, 2004), 5–6.

45. Larry Mercer, *A Gift from God: Foundational Principles of Biblical Parenting* (Chicago: Moody, 2001), 77–80.

Chapter 6 Caution—Prooftexting in Progress

1. Andee Seu, "Perseverance Pays: Taking the Wisdom of Woody to a New Level," *World* 16, no. 43 (November 10, 2001): 37.

2. Warren, *The Purpose Driven Life*, 325–26.

3. Ibid., 17, 20, 22.

4. Ibid., 30.

5. Isaiah 49:1–7 is the second in a series of four passages that describe this servant, along with 42:1–4 (which Matthew 12:17–21 quotes and applies to Jesus); 50:4–9; and 52:13–53:12. Note also the similarity between Isaiah 42:6 and 49:6.

6. See, for example, John R. W. Stott, *Between Two Worlds: The Art of Preaching in the Twentieth Century* (Grand Rapids: Eerdmans, 1982). W. Randolph Tate, *Biblical Interpretation: An Integrated Approach*, 3rd ed. (Peabody, MS: Hendrickson, 2008), structures his textbook according to three worlds—the worlds *behind* (a focus on the author), *within* (a focus on the text itself), and *in front of* (a focus on the reader) the text.

7. William A. Klein, Craig L. Blomberg, and Robert L. Hubbard Jr., *An Introduction to Biblical Interpretation*, rev. ed. (Nashville: Thomas Nelson, 2004), 482. These authors offer Satan's misuse of Psalm 91:11–12 in an effort to get Jesus to deliberately jump off the temple pinnacle as a biblical example of this application error (Matt. 4:5).

8. Jack Kuhatschek and Cindy Bunch, *How to Lead a Lifeguide Bible Study* (Downers Grove, IL: InterVarsity, 2002), 39. Their sixth question is: "What does this passage teach me about God, Jesus, myself, others?"

9. A book that completely ignores this issue is James R. Riddle, *The Complete Personalized Promise Bible: Every Promise in the Bible from Genesis to Revelation Personalized for You* (Tulsa, OK: Harrison House, 2004).

10. Ortlund, *Disciplines of the Beautiful Woman*, 71–72. She clarifies further: "Whether you're a long-time Bible student or a novice, the Holy Spirit is your personal teacher, and he will grade the material for you!"

11. M. Blaine Smith, *Should I Get Married?*, rev. ed. (Downers Grove, IL: InterVarsity, 2000), 76.

12. John H. Walton, *Genesis*, NIV Application Commentary (Grand Rapids: Zondervan, 2001), 178–79.

13. Richard G. Lee, ed., *The American Patriot's Bible: The Word of God and the Shaping of America* (Nashville: Nelson, 2009), 482.

14. Stan Huberfeld, *2 Chronicles 7:14 Revival* (Fort Washington, PA: Christian Literature Crusade, 2009). See also David Vesely's discussion of "God's View of 2 Chronicles 7:14" in *Righteousness Exalts a Nation: God's Love Will Change America* (Longwood, FL: Xulon, 2009), 57–65.

15. John Piper, "Testing the Use of 2 Chronicles 7:14," in *A Hunger for God: Desiring God through Fasting and Prayer* (Wheaton, IL: Crossway, 1997), 115–17.

16. Lois E. Lebar, *Education That Is Christian* (Wheaton, IL: Victor Books, 1989), 65.

17. For example, Herman Horne and Angus M. Gunn, *Jesus the Teacher: Examining His Expertise in Education*, rev. ed. (Grand Rapids: Kregel, 1998), originally published in 1920; Frank Webster Smith, *Jesus—Teacher: Principles of Education for Both Public and Bible School Teachers* (New York: Sturgis & Walton, 1916).

18. Lebar, *Education That Is Christian*, 66.

19. Frank Minirth, Don Hawkins, Paul Meier, and Richard Flournoy, *How to Beat Burnout: Help for Men and Women* (Chicago: Moody, 1986), 97.

20. Christina Maslach, *Burnout—The Cost of Caring* (Englewood Cliffs, NJ: Prentice-Hall, 1982), 3.

21. Minirth et. al, *How to Beat Burnout*, 14.

22. Ibid., 99–102.

23. James M. Houston, *In Pursuit of Happiness: Finding Genuine Fulfillment in Life* (Colorado Springs: NavPress, 1996), 174.

24. Daniel I. Block, *Book of Ezekiel: Chapters 1–24*, New International Commentary on the Old Testament (Grand Rapids: Eerdmans, 1997), 559–61. I held the traditional view until reading Block's defense of his interpretation.

25. Norman Vincent Peale, *Six Attitudes for Winners* (Carol Stream, IL: Tyndale House, 1989), 22–23.

26. Eldredge, *Wild at Heart*, 10–11, italics in original.

27. Ibid., 32–35.

28. Mark Buchanan, "In the Word: Stuck on the Road to Emmaus: The Secret to Why We Are Not Fulfilled," *Christianity Today* (July 12, 1999): 55.

29. Ibid., 57.

30. For an illustration of these last two warrants, see the discussion of 1 Samuel 25 on pages 91–92. It is clearly not the message of the text that we should call our spouse a "fool."

31. Warren, *The Purpose Driven Life*, 31.

32. Ibid.

33. Loren Cunningham with Janice Rogers, *Is That Really You, God? Hearing the Voice of God*, 2nd ed. (Seattle: YWAM, 2001), 155–56.

34. Bill Hamon, foreword to Sandie Freed, *Breaking the Threefold Demonic Cord: How to Discern and Defeat the Lies of Jezebel, Athaliah and Delilah* (Grand Rapids: Chosen Books, 2008), 11.

35. Freed, *Breaking the Threefold Demonic Cord*, 115–16. Unfortunately, Freed does not give the source for any of her name derivations.

36. Walter Kaiser Jr., *Toward an Exegetical Theology: Biblical Exegesis for Preaching and Teaching* (Grand Rapids: Baker, 1981), 152.

37. Warren Wiersbe, *God Isn't in a Hurry: Learning to Slow Down and Live* (Grand Rapids: Baker, 1994), 14.

Chapter 7 What's So Bad about "Textjacking"?

1. John Dunham, "High Fructose Scripture: Is Verse-by-Verse Bible Teaching Nutritious?," *Out of Ur*, June 5, 2007, http://www.outofur.com/archives/2007/06/high_fructose_s.html (accessed July 11, 2011). I prefer the term "textjacking" to "verse jacking," since this is a more inclusive term, even though the misuse of individual verses is more common than the misuse of larger discourse units.

2. Richard S. Briggs, *The Virtuous Reader: Old Testament Narrative and Interpretive Virtue*, Studies in Theological Interpretation (Grand Rapids: Baker, 2010).

3. The Qur'an repeatedly describes Jews and Christians as "people of the Book." See especially the thorough discussion in David L. Jeffrey, *People of the Book: Christian Identity and Literary Culture* (Grand Rapids: Eerdmans, 1996).

4. Bill Hamon, foreword to Sandie Freed, *Breaking the Threefold Demonic Cord*, 11. Freed, in turn, claims to have been given a dream or vision of hell to inspire her to write this book.

5. Christian Smith, *The Bible Made Impossible: Why Biblicism Is Not a Truly Evangelical Reading of Scripture* (Grand Rapids: Brazos, 2011), esp. chap. 1, "Biblicism and the Problem of Pervasive Interpretive Pluralism," 3–26. I share some of Smith's concerns but do not agree with his remedy for the problem.

6. Doug Ingram, *Ecclesiastes: A Peculiarly Postmodern Piece* (Cambridge: Grove Books, 2004), 23.

7. John Goldingay, *Models for Scripture* (Grand Rapids: Eerdmans, 1994), 346.

8. Ibid., emphasis added.

9. See, for example, Kevin J. Vanhoozer, "'But That's Your Interpretation': Realism, Reading, and Reformation," *Modern Reformation* (July/August 1999): 21–28.

10. Briggs, *Virtuous Reader*, 140.

11. Augustine, *On Christian Teaching* (1.36.40), trans. R. P. H. Green (Oxford: Oxford University Press, 1997), 27.

12. Briggs, *Virtuous Reader*, 142.

13. Augustine, *On Christian Teaching* (1.36.40), 27.

14. Ibid., 7.

15. This is the title of an anthology edited by New Testament scholar Greg K. Beale, *The Right Doctrine from the Wrong Texts: Essays on the Use of the Old Testament in the New* (Grand Rapids: Baker, 1994).

16. James W. Sire, *Scripture Twisting: 20 Ways the Cults Misread the Bible* (Downers Grove, IL: InterVarsity, 1980), esp. appendix 1, "A Brief Definition of Twenty Reading Errors," 155–60.

17. Manfred T. Brauch, *Abusing Scripture: The Consequences of Misreading the Bible* (Downers Grove, IL: InterVarsity, 2009), 15. Jacques Berlinerblau also speaks of abuses of the Bible in *Thumpin' It: The Use and Abuse of the Bible in Today's Presidential Politics* (Louisville: Westminster John Knox, 2008).

18. Dan B. Allender and Tremper Longman III, *Bold Love* (Colorado Springs: NavPress, 1992), 15. Jay Adams speaks similarly of those who "bend and warp the Word of God to fit ideas previously found in some pagan book" in "Biblical Interpretation and Counseling," *Journal of Biblical Counseling* 16 (1998): 7.

19. Willard M. Swartley offers detailed treatments of some of these issues in *Slavery, Sabbath, War, and Women: Case Issues in Biblical Interpretation* (Scottdale, PA: Herald, 1983).

20. Adams, "Biblical Interpretation and Counseling," 5.

Richard L. Schultz (PhD, Yale University) is the Blanchard Professor of Old Testament at Wheaton College. He is a regular contributor to scholarly journals and theological and biblical dictionary projects. He lives in Wheaton, Illinois.

ARE YOU SURE YOU KNOW WHAT YOUR FAVORITE BIBLE VERSES MEAN?

"This is a book that is long overdue, and I gladly commend it to you."
—Tim Challies, author and pastor

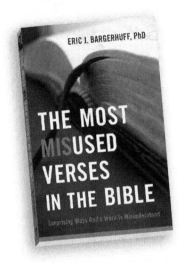

"I can do all things through Christ who strengthens me."**—Philippians 4:13**

"'For I know the plans I have for you,' declares the Lord, 'plans to prosper you and not to harm you, plans to give you hope and a future.'"**—Jeremiah 29:11**

"And we know that for those who love God all things work together for good."
—Romans 8:28

These and a surprising number of well-known Scripture passages are commonly misused or misunderstood. Even well-intentioned Christians take important verses out of context, and pastor Eric J. Bargerhuff has seen the effects: confusion, poor decisions, and a distorted view of God's Word.

In this concise yet thorough book, Bargerhuff helps all of us understand what these verses meant when they were written so we can apply them accurately today. Providing fascinating historical and scriptural insights, he shows how to read God's promises and instructions in context and appreciate even more the Bible's eternal message.

51974143R00097

Made in the USA
Lexington, KY
11 May 2016